D1576374

BRITISH STEAM
BR STANDARDS

This is a Perceptive Images 2012 © publication exclusively for Pen & Sword Books Ltd; which was compiled and edited by Keith Langston.

Additional editorial material was supplied by David Anderson, whose encouragement, railway knowledge and additional editorial material was invaluable.

Images supplied on a commercial basic by:
Colour Rail www.colour-rail.com
Rail Photoprints Collection www. www.railphotoprints.zenfolio.com
Transport Treasury www.transporttreasury.co.uk/

The author would also like to thank other accomplished photographers who have allowed their images to be used and they included; David Anderson, Michael Bentley, Graham Collier, Jonathan Clay, Crewe Works Archive, Roger Jermy, Dave Jones, Fred Kerr, Peter Kerslake/71000 Steam Locomotive Trust, Sue Langston, Len Mills, Mike Stokes Collection, Paul Pettitt and the 82045 Locomotive Trust.

BRITISH STEAM
BR STANDARDS

Keith Langston

WHARNCLIFFE
TRANSPORT

First published in Great Britain in 2012 by
Wharncliffe Transport
An imprint of
Pen & Sword Books Ltd
47 Church Street
Barnsley
South Yorkshire
S70 2AS

ISBN 978 1 84563 146 8

Cover image: BR Standard 'Class 5' No 73096 pictured hauling freight
on the Mid-Hants Railway. *Paul Pettitt*

Typeset in 11pt Minion by Mac Style, Beverley, East Yorkshire
Printed and bound in India by Replika Press Pvt. Ltd.

Pen & Sword Books Ltd incorporates the Imprints of Pen & Sword Aviation,
Pen & Sword Family History, Pen & Sword Maritime, Pen & Sword Military,
Pen & Sword Discovery, Wharncliffe Local History, Wharncliffe True Crime,
Wharncliffe Transport, Pen & Sword Select, Pen & Sword Military Classics,
Leo Cooper, The Praetorian Press, Remember When, Seaforth Publishing
and Frontline Publishing.

For a complete list of Pen & Sword titles please contact
PEN & SWORD BOOKS LIMITED
47 Church Street, Barnsley, South Yorkshire, S70 2AS, England
E-mail: enquiries@pen-and-sword.co.uk
Website: www.pen-and-sword.co.uk

CONTENTS

Built at Crewe Works in 1954 BR Standard Class 8P 4-6-2 No 71000 DUKE OF GLOUCESTER was described as being the ultimate in British steam locomotive design. In revenue earning BR service the Caprotti configured locos performance fell well short of expectations. However following comprehensive engineering improvements made during its preserved life the Derby designed express passenger locomotive has more than justified a 'Best of British' accolade. *Keith Langston*

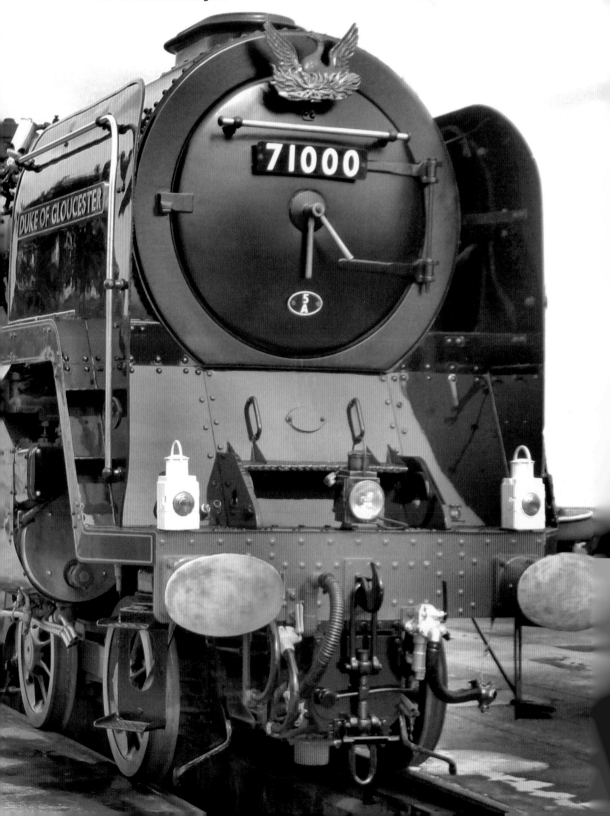

ROBERT ARTHUR RIDDLES C.B.E.

Chosen to lead the team set up in order to create the Standard Class locomotives was Robert Arthur Riddles (born in 1892) who trained as an apprentice with London North Western Railway (LNWR) at Crewe Works between 1909 and 1913, at the onset of the First World War he joined the Royal Engineers serving until 1919. His first two senior positions within the railway industry were firstly Assistant to the Works Manager Crewe and then Progress Assistant to the Works Manager Crewe between 1920 and 1928. Thereafter Riddles

Riddles 9F 2-10-0 BR Standard No 92224 is pictured hard at work approaching Oxford in 1964, built at Crewe in 1958 this locomotive was withdrawn in September 1967. The 9Fs were the last of the BR Standards to be built and were thought by many railwaymen to be Riddles most successful design. *David Anderson*

served at Derby in the position of Assistant Works Superintendent before returning to Crewe in order to fulfil the same roll. In 1933 he became Locomotive Assistant to the celebrated locomotive engineer W. A. Stanier (C.M.E LMS) and progressed to become Principal Assistant to the C.M.E, a roll he continued in until 1937 when for a two year spell he became Mechanical and Electrical Engineer L.M.S. Scotland.

In 1939, just prior to the start of the Second World War, Riddles was in the United States of America as leader of the LMS contingent accompanying the Coronation Scot exhibition train on its tour of that country. Following the end of the tour, which culminated with a visit to the New York Worlds Fair, Riddles was instructed to oversee arrangements to bring the locomotive (6229 alias 6220) and its luxury train back to Britain. However the outbreak of the war in Europe left the streamlined locomotive and its train stranded in the USA, the loco eventually returning home in 1940, however the carriages stayed in the USA until the end of hostilities.

On his return to the UK Riddles was appointed to the roll of Director of Transportation Equipment, Ministry of Supply and in 1941 became Deputy Director General of that organisation. In 1943 he returned to the L.M.S. as Chief Stores Superintendent and was in that year awarded the C.B.E. Riddles was promoted first to Vice President Engineering in 1946 and then to Chief Mechanical and Electrical Engineer for British Railways in 1948. He retired on 30th September 1953 and died in June 1983.

Director of Transportation and Equipment, Ministry of Supply 1939–1943

To look forward it is sometimes appropriate to take a cursory glance backwards and in the case of Britain's railways to the events of 1939 – 1945. To operate for the common good, and with cohesion, the four railway companies and their sub-sidiary operations were placed directly under government control. The control order was made on September 1st, 1939, under the Emergency Powers (Defence) Act, 1939.

Official statistics collated in 1943 illustrate not only the importance of the railway network to the country but also the enormity and complexity of the network. The 19,624 route miles when translated into single miles and counting sidings, loops etc totalled an 'actual' 59,958 miles of standard gauge track (4ft 8½ ins) controlling movements on which were some 10,300 signal boxes.

The number of sleepers to one mile of track was recorded as 2,112. Over 1½ million cubic yards of stone ballast, and several hundreds of thousands of tons of steel rails were required annually. All carriage types totalled 45,838 vehicles collectively providing 2.65 million seats, whilst over I.25 million railway wagons and 17,318 containers were in service. There were some 7000 passenger stations which were augmented by 6900 goods stations.

Enormous tonnages of freight were carried, e.g. the weekly total of coal moved by the railways averaged 4 million tons which was approximately 80% of all that

'Austerities' on shed at Langwith (41J) and still serviceable in September 1963, although when built they were only anticipated to have a relatively short working life. Loco No 90088 was built by the NBL and entered service in October 1944 as No 63088 and was scrapped in November 1965 whilst No 90411 was built by the same company and entered service in February 1945 as No 78538 being scrapped in November 1964. *Keith Langston*

produced. The postal service was almost entirely dependant on the railways for trunk movements and over 25 million mailbags and 90 million parcels were annually moved by train. In addition to rail vehicles the companies owned approximately 35,000 horse and motor vehicles and 130 steam ships.

The Ministry of Supply quickly embraced the challenge that the war would require more steam locomotives to be built not just for use in the UK but also for shipping overseas, a shortage of time and the need to control costs were crucial factors. As a matter of some urgency Riddles set to work overseeing the design and construction of new 2-8-0 and 2-10-0 locomotives which became known as 'The Austerities'. In 1943 a total of 150 Riddles 'War Department' 2-10-0 locomotives were built by the North British Locomotive Company of Glasgow and between 1943 and 1946 a total of 934 Riddles 'War Department' 2-8-0 locomotives were build by the North British Locomotive Company of Glasgow (NBL) and Vulcan Foundry of Newton le Willows (VF).

The 'S160 Class' 2-8-0 locomotives were a standard design used by the US Army Transportation Corps (USATC), and shipped to Britain during World War 2 in large numbers ready for the Invasion of France in 1944. Prior to the invasion, they were used by all four of Britain's main railway companies. Pictured is No 3278 a preserved example which carries the name FRANKLIN D. ROOSEVELT, it is usually located on the Mid Hants Railway. *Keith Langston*

As part of the motive power wartime requirements the Ministry of Supply also selected the standard six coupled (0-6-0) Hunslet Engine Companies saddle tank for production with some modifications as a war time shunting engine. To further help overcome the motive power shortages the Ministry of Supply purchased a batch of 2-8-0 locomotives from the USA. Known as S160 Class they were designed by Major J W. Marsh of the US Army Corps of Engineers and built in the USA by locomotive builders Baldwin, Alco and Lima.

The Standard Design Group

In 1948 British Railways under the auspices of the British Transport Commission (BTC) set about the mammoth task of modernising the countries steam locomotive fleet. A new organisation called the Standard Design Group was created and given

The Standard Design Group was charged with introducing a new series of easily maintained locomotives with common design features. 3MT 2-6-2T BR Standard 'Class 3 Tank' is pictured under construction in the Swindon Works erecting shop during September 1954. Entering BR service in November 1954 this loco was scrapped in December 1964 when just 10 years and one month old. *Keith Langston Collection*

a clear mandate to solve the operational problems caused by steam motive power shortages across the regions. They were to do so by introducing a new series of easily maintained locomotives with common design features.

In the first instance the 'Group' set about evaluating the engines of the old Big Four in order to decide which, if any, of their characteristics would be of use in the planned new designs. To help in the decision making process locomotive exchanges between the regions of British Railways took place, during which a very comprehensive amount of operating and performance related data was collected. In the final analysis of all the locomotive designs which were trialled the Stanier designed locomotives (of the former LMS) were said to have impressed the groups team leader the most.

Riddles communicated with the other members of the design group through a committee of Regional Chief Draughtsmen chaired by Ernest Stewart Cox. Riddles made clear his design requirements and aims which he categorised thus......

- 'The upmost in steam producing capacity permitted by weight and clearance restrictions'.
- 'Simplicity, visibility and accessibility, with the number of moving parts reduced to a minimum'.
- 'Proportions of all types of engines designed to give the widest possible range of mixed traffic working'.
- 'Increased life of bearings by the use of roller bearings for all wheels when financially justified, and otherwise of generously proportioned plain bearings with manganese liners'.

Ease of locomotive disposal was high on the list of Riddles requirements for the new steam locomotive fleet. This picture, no doubt posed in order to show how easily ash pan emptying could be achieved on the 9Fs was taken to help illustrate that point. Note however the clean smock coat, front gloved hand and highly polished shoes of the supposed locoman, the reader could be excused for thinking that the gentleman had not just 'worked in' the loco! *Keith Langston Collection*

One of Riddles eight basic BR Standard design requirements was '*Reduction to a minimum of slipping by the use of as high factors of adhesion as possible, and of sensitive regulators and efficient sanding gear*'. Of course fulfilling that requirement depended on the skill of the footplate crew and the condition of the track. The fireman of 4-6-0 5MT BR Standard 'Class 5' No 73092 can only sit and watch as a proportion of his fire is propelled up the chimney as the engine slips violently during his driver's attempt at a quick getaway from London Waterloo in this 1966 picture! This 1955 Derby built loco was scrapped in January 1968. *Keith Langston Collection*

- 'Simplification of shed maintenance by increased use of mechanical lubricators and grease lubrication'.
- 'Reduction in disposal time at sheds by the fitting of self cleaning smoke boxes, rocking grates and self-emptying ash pans'.
- 'Reduction to a minimum of slipping by the use of as high factors of adhesion as possible, and of sensitive regulators and efficient sanding gear'.
- 'Within the foregoing requirements, the promotion of maximum thermal efficiency by large firegrate area, to assure low rates of combustion in average working conditions, coupled with long-lap valve gear and high temperature superheat'.

For reasons of simplicity and low cost all the originally proposed standard types were to be constructed as 2-cylinder locomotives. Riddles subscribed to the belief that if all other factors were equal a 2-cylinder steam engine, with 4 beats per revolution, promoted better steaming. As will be seen later locomotive No 71000 DUKE OF GLOUCESTER was to become the only exception to the BR Standard 2-cylinder rule.

Brighton designed and built 4MT 2-6-4T BR Standard 'Class 4 Tank' No 80072 is posed partly restored in the erecting shop at Crewe Works during the September 2005 'Great Gathering' event, the now completed locomotive is based at the Llangollen Railway. This locomotive entered traffic in November 1953 and was withdrawn by BR in July 1965. *Keith Langston*

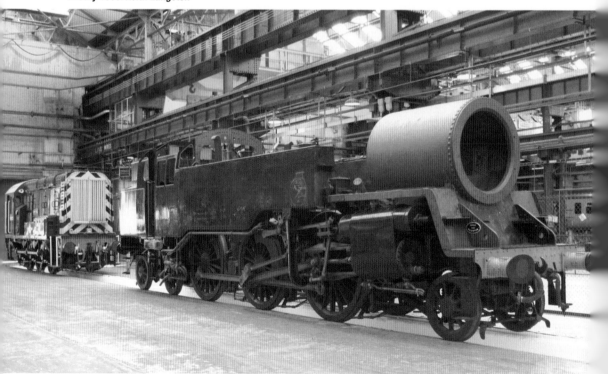

Following the aforementioned 1948 Locomotive Exchange Trials and the assessment of data from the various regional offices a programme of work was introduced and the outlined tasks were then divided between the headquarters drawing offices of previous 'Big Four' companies, namely Brighton, Derby, Doncaster and Swindon. However the Standard Design Group did not allocated responsibility for complete specific locomotives to any one office. Instead each of the four offices was made responsible for the preparation of drawings for particular 'Standard' components in respect of all the engines with the allocated responsibilities being detailed thus;

Brighton: Brakes and sanding gear.
Derby: Bogies and trucks; tenders; wheels; tyres; axles and spring gear.
Doncaster: Coupling and connecting rods; valve gear and cylinder details.
Swindon: Boiler and smokebox details; steam fittings.

In addition each of the design centres was designated as 'parent' for one or more of the standard types and charged with producing the relevant locomotive general arrangement drawings. Varying numbers of the 12 individual BR Standard Class locomotives were built at Brighton, Crewe, Darlington, Derby, Doncaster, Horwich and Swindon locomotive works. In total 999 Standard Class engines were built between 1951 and 1958, of those 769 were tender engines and 230 tank engines.

BRITISH RAILWAYS STANDARD CLASS LOCOMOTIVES

Introduction

The strains of maintaining intensive services during World War II (1939–1945) had taken its toll on the countries ageing locomotive fleet. Even though electrification and dieselization developments in other European countries were being observed, and widely discussed by UK railway engineers the newly formed transport undertaking, named British Railways (BR) and formed on January 1st 1948, had very definite plans of their own. Although mindful of the new advances in traction technology BR nevertheless made the decision to continue operating steam locomotives, at least in the short term.

British Railways came into being on January 1st 1948, following Royal Assent being given to the Transport Act 1947. The four railway companies which were created in 1923, London Midland & Scottish Railway (L.M.S.R.) London North Eastern Railway (L.N.E.R.) Great Western Railway (G.W.R.) and Southern Railway (S.R.) then became one entity with overall responsibility for the then mainly steam operated railway network. The property and rolling stock of the four companies was re-branded and administratively six regions within BR were created. They were the London Midland Region, Eastern Region, North Eastern Region, Scottish Region, Southern Region and the Western Region.

In 1948 the railways employed approximately 648,740 staff and at that time operated just over 20,000 standard gauge steam locomotives. A very large percentage of the engines were approaching the end of their useful working lives whilst a great many others were in poor shape having only been maintained to a minimum standard due to the severe restrictions imposed by wartime operating

When first introduced the BR Standard Class locomotives represented a totally different design concept with perhaps the most noticeable feature of the tender engine types being the 'American style' high running plate located well clear of the wheels and motion. BR 4MT 4-6-0 No 75006 is pictured at Swindon in October 1951, the loco was then only one month old. This engine almost served to the end of steam on BR being withdrawn in August 1967. *KCH Fairey/Colour Rail*

conditions. If the country was to revitalise its economy it would need industry to provide the catalyst for growth and the railways would therefore need to play a crucial part. A new breed of steam locomotives was urgently required.

To correct the motive power imbalance British Railways decided to embark upon a programme of steam locomotive building from 1951 onwards, whilst at the same time withdrawing from service large numbers of older engines. As time has shown the locomotives which became collectively known as the BR Standard Classes were in fact only a stop gap measure, indeed various examples were in BR service for less than 10 years and others for as little as 5 years. The new locomotives were allocated numbers between 70000 and 92250 by BR. Within that series were locomotives with numbers 90000 to 90731 and 90750 to 90774 which were Ministry of Supply (War Department) 'Austerity' locomotives which saw service in all regions of BR and their details are also included in this publication.

Chapter 1

7P6F (7MT) 4-6-2 BR STANDARD 'BRITANNIA'

First of the 999 BR Standard Class locomotives, 4-6-2 No 70000 BRITANNIA is pictured at Neasden (24E) en-route to Marylebone Station London for an official BR inspection and naming ceremony, by the then Minister of Transport Alfred Barnes MP on 30th January 1951.

Having been first out-shopped in un-lined black and without nameplates No 70000 was repainted into BR passenger green with, black and orange lining, a red background to the nameplate and a bright metal finish to the wheel rims, handrails, buffers and drawgear prior to the ceremony.

The 'Britannia' livery was eventually changed to BR unlined green without bright metal fittings. For many years the cab roof of BRITANNIA was painted white to commemorate the loco hauling the funeral train of HRH King George VI from Norfolk to London, following his death at Sandringham in February 1952. *Colour Rail*

B R Standard 'Britannia Class' was the first of the 999 'Riddles' Standard type locomotives to enter service. The first of the class 70000 BRITANNIA was rolled out of Crewe Locomotive Works in January 1951. The new class of 55 engines were considered at the time to be a striking design of Mixed Traffic locomotives, intended to have wide route availability. The Britannias were roughly equal in power to the Western Region (ex GWR) Castle class, the London Midland Region (ex LMS) Royal Scot class, the Southern Region (ex SR) West Country class and the Eastern Region (ex LNER) V2 class.

The 4-6-2 locomotives were designed in the Derby drawing office of BR and all were built at Crewe. They were given the number series 70000 to 70054 with 70000 to 70024 entering service in 1951, 70025 to 70044 entering service in 1952/53 and 70045 to 70054 entering service in 1954.

The Britannia boiler was designated BR1 type and its proportions were comparable with those of Gresley's widely acclaimed V2 boiler, which had proved to be an excellent steam producer. The BR1 was superheated and in keeping with Standard Design Group policy was fitted with a self-cleaning smokebox, rocking grate and self-emptying ashpan. To complete the 'new' look Riddles added roller bearings and a tender cab. The new Pacific class was claimed by many observers at the time to have a distinctive 'LMS look' to it.

The 'Britannia' build specification took into all general aspects the Standard Design Groups criteria and in addition called for a liberal number of wash out plugs and doors, an enhanced design of regulator in the smokebox and improved accessibility of injectors and all pipe work. Importance was also placed on providing the enginemen with a better and more spacious cab/tender layout. In fact Riddles

Britannia Class Facts

BR Pacific 'Britannia' Class 7P6F (7MT) 4-6-2

Built: Crewe Works 1951–54, 54 locomotives built.

Loco Weight: 94 tons 0 cwt

Tenders: BR1 49 tons 3 cwt, BR1A 52 tons 10 cwt, BR1D 54 tons 10 cwt

Driving Wheels Diameter: 6 foot 2 inches

Boiler Pressure: 250lb/psi

Cylinders: (2) 20 inch diameter x 28 inch stroke

Valve Gear: (piston valves) Walschaerts

Coal Capacity: BR1 and BR1A 7 tons, BR1D 9 tons

Water Capacity: BR1 4250 gallons, BR1A 5000 gallons, and BR1D 4725 gallons

Tractive Effort: 32,150lb at (85% pressure)

insisted that a wooden mock up of the proposed cab design be exhibited to staff prior to the intended design being signed off.

The Riddles Class 7 'Pacific' was intended as a fast mixed traffic locomotive with wide route availability. The small (by express locomotive standards) 6ft 2in diameter driving wheels underlined the designer's mixed traffic intentions, whilst their low axle loading (a little over 20 tons) satisfied route availability criteria. In addition the wheelbase of 58ft 3in meant that the class could easily be turned on the many 60ft turntables in use around the regions. The locomotives' length over buffers was specified to be 68ft 9in.

The tractive effort of the 'Britannia' class was listed at 32,150lb (at 85% boiler pressure) compared with for example the rebuilt 'Royal Scot' class listed at 33,150lb (at 85% boiler pressure). At the time double blastpipes were seen as the norm for large locomotives, therefore observers were surprised by the 'Standard' team's choice of single blastpipe and chimney. Riddles foresaw that the choice of just two 20in x 28in cylinders would appreciably reduce maintenance cost/time, in comparison to multi-cylinder locomotives.

Performance did not suffer either as the class constantly proved capable of maintaining express timings, often with heavily loaded trains. When in the care of a locomotive crew who had taken the time to learn the required technique of handling the two-cylinder 'Pacific's', performances more normally associated with multi-cylinder 'Class 8' steam power were regularly recorded.

Locomotives Nos 70000 to 70034 and 70050 to 70054 were fitted with roller bearings and thereafter engines Nos 70035 to 70039 were built with roller bearings fitted only on the leading and trailing coupled axles, in another deviation from original design specification loco Nos 70040 to 70049 were built with plain bearings throughout. Reportedly experience in traffic showed no great advantage with roller bearings when judged by either reliability or cost criteria.

Initial locomotive allocations for operating purposes:

Nos. 70000–70014   Eastern Region
Nos. 70015–70024   Western Region
Nos. 70025–70029   Western Region
Nos. 70030–70044   London Midland Region
Nos. 70045–70049   London Midland Region
Nos. 70050–70054   Scottish Region

However, in practice some early alterations took place with extra locomotives being reallocated to the Eastern Region and some to the Southern Region.

Initial Problems in Traffic

The class leader BRITANNIA suffered a failure on only its second revenue earning trip when on 2 February 1951, the loco blew out its right hand cylinder cover and piston head. The loco was very quickly repaired but some 12 days later a similar failure happened, to the loco's left hand cylinder. Investigations revealed that a partial failure within the engine's steam drier had caused incidents of water 'carry over' into the cylinders. Later problems associated with water carry over affected the first batch of engines with the flat design of steam dome (with a 'smaller' valve) being identified as the cause of the problems.

Further problems in traffic were reported as the first batch of locos entered revenue earning service. In fact the first 25 locos were temporarily withdrawn in October/November 1951 in order to rectify the fact that driving wheels had

Locomotive No 70000 BRITANNIA is pictured under construction at Crewe Works. This picture shows clearly the original cab design (later changed) it is easy to see that the entire footplate was an extension of the cab floor backwards to the front face of the tender. There was no 'fall plate' and the floor was supported by cantilever brackets extending from the firebox. *Crewe Works Archive*

reportedly 'shifted' on their axles. Initial concerns were raised even higher after loco No 70004 WILLIAM SHAKESPEARE suffered a snapped connecting rod whilst travelling at speed near Headcorn in Kent; furthermore 6 other instances of con-rod failure within the early production batch of the new class were reported. The fault was traced to the method used to fit the roller bearings onto the axles, and after modifications all 25 engines were returned to traffic by early 1952.

Notwithstanding the earlier reported teething problems the Britannia design was generally considered to be a complete success and when first in service (after the aforementioned modifications) the type put in some memorable performances on the former Great Eastern Railway main line into East Anglia, as a result of which timings on those routes were appreciably improved. They were however not at first well received on the BR Western Region where the left-hand driving position was at variance with standard practice on ex GWR territory, a point perchance overlooked by the locomotive's designers?

Modifications

As mentioned earlier problems with the design of the steam dome had also created instances of cylinder damage caused by 'water carry over', the design of the dome was modified (made larger) to incorporate a bigger valve, which reportedly cured those faults. In addition the new 'dome' design was then incorporated into the production run.

Initially the main driving wheel return cranks were a copy of the London North Eastern Railway (LNER) 'block type', which had been used by Arthur Peppercorn on his A1 and A2 class engines. Later the crank design was changed to a simpler design of London Midland Scottish Railway (LMSR) four stud fitting in order to simplify maintenance and eliminate problems of heating associated with the bearings situated within the cranks.

The original design also specified that a fluted type of coupling and connecting rods should be used however over time the class of locos had their driving wheel coupling rods replaced with tapered rectangular section rods (aka fish bellied rods).In traffic the original design of milled rods (so machined to form the flutes) were proved to be intrinsically weak and it was determined that they had contributed to incidents of coupling rods breaking when driving wheels slipped at high speeds.

To help with servicing a sustainably built step on the front buffer beam was constructed. Initially the locomotives had small individual foot steps welded to each of the angled uprights below the smokebox door. Loco No 70045 LORD ROWALLAN was fitted with LMS style oval buffers following a repair after collision damage, all of the other engines had round buffers.

Locomotives Nos. 70043 LORD KITCHENER and 70044 EARL HAIG were delivered new with dual braking. The Westinghouse air brake compressor gear was

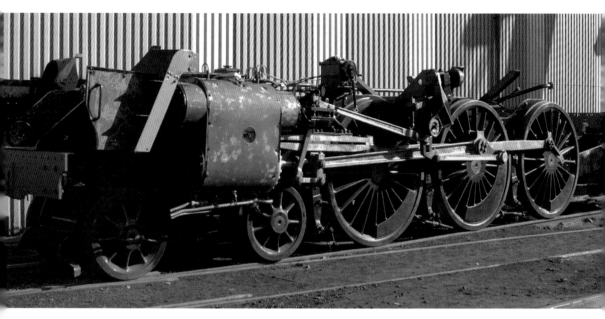

The rolling chassis of No 70000 seen in 2009 at LNWR Heritage Ltd Crewe shows clearly the difference in profile of the original fluted style connecting rods and the modified design of rectangular section 'fish bellied' driving wheel coupling rods. *Keith Langston*

located either side of the smokebox, initially prohibiting the use of smoke deflectors on those locomotives. The associated air reservoirs were attached to the running plate. The system was tested on mineral and express passenger trains and after the trials the gear was removed and the engines fitted with smoke deflectors and then given their allocated names.

Locomotive crews had complained about footplate draughts on the early batch of engines and to combat that draught screens were fitted between the engine and tender. On later built engines modifications were carried out in order to better address the problem by improving the cab-tender interface. Several types of tender were fitted and the table below shows the original pairings.

Loco numbers	Tender type	Water capacity	Coal Capacity
70000–70024	BR1	4250 gallon	7 tons
70025–70029	BR1A	5000 gallon	7 tons
70030–70044	BR1	4250 gallon	7 tons
70045–70054	BR1D	4725 gallons	9 tons

Note the BR1D tenders were straight sided and incorporated steam operated coal pushers, they also had a shortened tender handrail.

By the early months of 1964 the rapid spread of dieselisation was starting to force the 7MT Pacific locos away from the Western and Eastern Regions and, during the

Newly rebuilt Britannia Pacific No 70000 is pictured as the loco crew 'wait for the road' northbound at Crewe on 9 November 2010, the occasion of the 7MT locomotives first mainline trial. LNWR Works Manager Steve Latham is stood in the cab door and to the right of him the folded concertina type draught screen can be seen. *Graham Collier*

remainder of that year all 55 of the class were allocated to the London Midland Region, with all but seven being sent to Carlisle Kingmoor (12A) depot.

The first of the class to be scrapped was No 70007 COEUR-DE-LION which was cut up at Crewe in July 1965, having worked in BR service for only 14 years. By the year end of 1966 just 42 of the class were still in use and only one locomotive (No 70013) survived in service until the end of BR steam.

Originally BR intended to preserve No 70000 BRITANNIA as part of the national collection but then dropped that plan following vandalism of that locomotive whilst it was stored in their safe keeping! The British Railways Board then alternatively chose No 70013 OLIVER CROMWELL for the collection, as a result of which that loco was overhauled and repainted at Crewe Works in January 1967.

The engine was then returned to traffic hauling special trains right up to the end of steam on BR, including the final leg of a Farewell to Steam special from

Locomotive No 70013 OLIVER CROMWELL pictured in pristine ex works condition at Doncaster (36A) in May 1959. The replacement tapered rectangular section coupling rods (aka fish bellied rods) can clearly be identified.
Colour Rail

Manchester to Carlisle on 11th August 1968. As good fortune would have it locomotive No 70000 BRITANNIA was eventually preserved after being privately purchased. Both Britannia class 7MT Pacific locomotives were again returned to service during 2011 and are set to haul mainline special trains during the life of their respective 10 year boiler certificates, and thereafter hopefully beyond that period pending refurbishment.

To facilitate the haulage of modern mainline stock restored locomotive No 70000 BRITANNIA has been fitted with air brake equipment, the pump for that can be seen located inside the nearside smoke deflector. The associated air storage tanks are located under the loco's tender. *Keith Langston*

Naming the locomotives

From 1948 until the mid 1950s the responsibility for selecting steam locomotive names rested with the specially created Locomotive Naming Committee which consisted of three senior railway officials of the time. They were Ernest Stewart Cox, George Dow, and committee chairman Derek Barrie.

The committee first set itself several rules and over their period in power developed a way of working to suit the British Railways hierarchy. They were insistent that any name selected had to be, in their terms, 'euphonious in nature'. In plain English the chosen names had to be possessed of an agreeable sound! These criteria attached to name selection, although applied no doubt for deadly serious reasons, can with the passage of time perchance be viewed in a humorous light. Imagine if you will, one of the 'Euphonic Three' pacing the committee room with his back ramrod straight, forearms extended and hands open in an encompassing theatrical manner, whilst reciting out loud a name under consideration. In order to gauge the magnitude of the euphonious effect, from the reaction of his colleagues!

Importantly the committee also ruled that names should have a meaning which would be readily understood by any interested party, be they railway connected or simply members of the public. Whilst the committee made known a preference for names of heroes and historically important people they stated that they were keen to resist names or associations with the military, possibly because of a desire to make a new start following the then recent ending of hostilities. Their first task was to choose names for Britannia Class locomotives, 54 of the 55 engines in the class were given names and interestingly that list did however include names with military connections.

Getting started was perhaps the greatest challenge and choosing a suitable name for locomotive No 70000 caused great debate, not just amongst the committee but also across the wider British Railways executive family. The name BRITANNIA came not from the 'Euphonic Three' or even a member of the railway executive but perhaps fittingly from a member of the Great British public. The gentleman credited with putting that suggestion forward was none other than the accomplished railway photographer, and much loved enthusiast Bishop Eric Treacy (*1907–1978*).

The name BRITANNIA was already in use and was carried by LMS Jubilee Class loco No 45700. The naming committee had a policy of not using names already allocated or in use on other locomotives. However as the recommended name met with the approval of both R.A. Riddles and G.S. Hussey (as it commemorated the Britannia and Lion emblem of the London & North Western Railway LNWR) the committee were overruled. Accordingly the 1936 Crewe built Jubilee locomotive was renamed AMETHYST in September 1951.The railway Bishop's excellent suggestion most certainly did fit all the criteria and it set the theme of a naming process which featured amongst its number many great Britons.

Other subjects were also chosen for the origin of names and additionally those locomotives originally allocated to the BR Scottish Region were given the names of

When first out shopped from Crewe Works, in January 1951 No 70000 carried an unlined all black livery which was in keeping with the ruling BR livery policy of the time for Mixed Traffic locomotives (no nameplate was carried during that period). The more familiar lined 'BR Green' express passenger livery was applied just prior to the official naming ceremony. The loco is pictured in all black livery at the works of LNWR Heritage Ltd Crewe after being restored to working order in 2010. *Keith Langston*

The Britannia class locomotives carried their names on the smoke deflectors, National Collection preserved loco No 70013 OLIVER CROMWELL is pictured outside the workshops at LNWR Heritage Ltd during a 2011 visit for firebox repairs. It can be seen that the loco carries a later style of BR Midland smoke deflectors, without a full set of handrails. The letters SC under the 12A (Carlisle Kingmoor) shed plate indicates that the loco has a 'Self Cleaning Smokebox'. That was comprised of a wire-mesh device fitted inside the smokebox which causes most of the 'char' blown through the boiler tubes to be thrown out of the chimney during travel, rather than it collecting in a heap in the smokebox. *Keith Langston*

selected Scottish 'Firths' whilst BR Western Region engines took on some of the names formerly allocated to Churchward's 'Star' class 4-6-0s. Many of the locomotive naming ceremonies were carried out at various railway stations around the British Railways network.

7P6F/7MT 4-6-2 BR Standard 'Britannia' class

70000 BRITANNIA built Crewe Works, entered service January 1951 with a BR1 4250 gallon tender, withdrawn from BR service June 1966. This locomotive is preserved and is in private ownership.

Britannia is the ancient term for *Great Britain* and also the female personification of the island. The name is Latin and was derived from the Greek form *Prettanike* or *Brettaniai* which originally referred to the collection of individually named islands, which included *Great Britain (Albion).* After their AD 43 conquest of Britain the Romans also named their new established province *Britannia.* The Latin name *Britannia* long survived the 5th century Roman withdrawal from Britain and the eventual fall of the *Roman Empire* becoming Britain in English and Prydain in modern Welsh. In the 2nd century *Roman Britannia* came to be personified as a goddess, and was thereafter depicted armed with a trident, shield and wearing a centurion's helmet. In that form 'she' is still depicted on some British decimal coins of the modern era.

Privately owned preserved BR Standard Britannia class 4-6-2 No 70000 BRITANNIA is pictured passing Gaerwen signal box on the Bangor to Holyhead section of the North Wales Coast main line with a recreated 'Irish Mail' special Crewe–Holyhead–Crewe run during July 1992. *Dave Jones*

It was always the intention of BR to operate the Britannia Class 4-6-2s as 'Mixed Traffic' locomotives. Class leader BRITANNIA is pictured on such a duty at Wolvercot Junction, Oxford with an Oxford (Cowley) – Birmingham (Longbridge) car transporter train in this 1963 image. *David Anderson*

From the time it was withdrawn from BR service, and restored to back mainline condition 'Standard Britannia' No 70000 BRITANNIA has been a firm favorite with charter operators and enthusiasts alike. The loco has appeared in many regions of the UK and also regularly visits preserved railways. In this June 1994 image the engine was pictured approaching Abergele (ex Holyhead) on the North Wales coast route. In 2010 No 70000 began a further 10 year period of mainline operation following a rebuild at LNWR Heritage Ltd Crewe. *Fred Kerr*

70001 LORD HURCOMB built Crewe Works, entered service January 1951 with a BR1 4250 gallon tender, withdrawn from BR service August 1966. Cut for scrap by Motherwell Machinery & Scrap, Wishaw in December 1966/January 1967.

Cyril William Hurcomb, 1st Baron Hurcomb GCB, KBE (1883 – 1975) was a British civil servant. Lord Hurcomb was head of the *Ministry of War Transport* and the first chairman of the *British Transport Commission* (BTC) which he served between 1948 and 1953. His Lordship was a very keen ornithologist; accordingly he played a key role in formulating and putting into law the *1954 Protection of Birds Act*. He served for a period as chairman of the *Royal Society for the Protection of Birds* and went on to become president of that society. He was elevated to the peerage as Baron Hurcomb in July 1950.

BR Standard Britannia 7MT 4-6-2 No 70001 LORD HURCOMB makes a fine sight as 'she' thunders through Wickham Market station with steam to spare, in this undated 1950s image. This railway station is actually located in the village of Campsea Ashe, Suffolk and stands on the Ipswich-Lowestoft East Suffolk Line and is some 2 miles from Wickham Market. *Dr Ian C. Allen/Transport Treasury*

70002 GEOFFREY CHAUCER built Crewe Works, entered service March 1951 with a BR1 4250 gallon tender, withdrawn from BR service January 1967. Cut for scrap by Campbells of Airdrie in May/June 1967.

Geoffrey Chaucer (circa. 1343–1400), was known as *the Father of English Literature*, and is considered by some to be the greatest English poet of the *'Middle Ages'*. He was the first poet to have been buried in *Poet's Corner of Westminster Abbey*. While he achieved fame during his lifetime as an author, philosopher, alchemist and astronomer Chaucer also maintained an active career in the civil service as a bureaucrat, courtier and diplomat. He is perhaps best loved today for his work The *Canterbury Tales*. Chaucer was a crucial figure in developing the legitimacy of the vernacular, *Middle English*, at a time when the dominant literary languages in England were French and Latin.

BR Standard Britannia 7MT 4-6-2 No 70002 GEOFFREY CHAUCER is seen passing through Kirkstall, Leeds with a parcel train comprised of mixed vans. The loco is minus its nameplates in this image taken on 20 August 1966, but even so the young enthusiast seen on the top of the wall is still busy noting the engine's details. This loco was withdrawn from service by BR six months after this picture was taken, in January 1967 but not cut for scrap until June of that year. *Mike Stokes Collection*

70003 JOHN BUNYAN built Crewe Works, entered service March 1951 with a BR1 4250 gallon tender, withdrawn from BR service March 1967. Cut for scrap by Campbells of Airdrie November/December 1967.

John Bunyan (1628–1688) was a puritanical English born *Christian* writer and preacher, famous for writing *Pilgrim's Progress*. Bunyan led what could best be described as a varied and eventful life during which he served in the Parliamentarian army at Newport Pagnell garrison during the English Civil War. His beliefs, writings and preachings brought him to the notice of those in power and as his popularity, and indeed notoriety, described by his detractors as a witch, a Jesuit and a highwayman and accused of many things including infidelity and polygamy. Bunyan suffered imprisonment for his beliefs on several occasions and indeed wrote part of *Pilgrims Progress* whilst in Bedford Goal. *The Pilgrim's Progress* is arguably one of the most widely known ever written. Extensively translated it is said that Protestant missionaries commonly translated it as the first thing after the Bible.

BR Standard Britannia 7MT No 70003 JOHN BUNYAN at Norwich after arriving with an RCTS railtour entitled 'Commemoration of Great Eastern Steam', which originated in London and ran on 31 March 1962. Note the original design handrails have been removed from the smoke deflectors and replaced with two handholds and a short horizontal handrail. The later style of 'fish bellied' rectangular section main driving rods can be identified in this image. *Rail Photoprints Collection*

70004 WILLIAM SHAKESPEARE built Crewe Works, entered service March 1951 with a BR1 4250 gallon tender, withdrawn from BR service December 1967. Cut for scrap by Wards of Inverkeithing March/April 1968.

William Shakespeare (1564–1616) was a poet and playwright, widely regarded as the greatest writer in the English language and the world's pre-eminent dramatist. He is often referred to as the *Bard of Avon* and also called *England's National Poet*. Shakespeare was born and brought up in *Stratford-upon-Avon* where at the age of 18, he married *Anne Hathaway*, with whom he had three children. His plays have been translated into every major living language and they are said to be performed more often than those of any other playwright. Between 1585 and 1592, he began working in London as an actor, writer, and part owner of a playing company called the *Lord Chamberlain's Men* (later to be known as the *King's Men*). Retiring to his birth town circa 1613 he died there some three years later. In modern times some have cast doubt on whether or not the 'Actor' was really also a prolific writer!

BR Standard Britannia 7MT No 70004 WILLIAM SHAKESPEARE is pictured 'on shed' at Stockport Edgeley (9B) on 30 June 1966, note that although the engine remained in service until November 1967 the nameplates have already been removed. *Keith Langston*

70005 JOHN MILTON built Crewe Works, entered service April 1951 with a BR1 4250 gallon tender, withdrawn from BR service July 1967. Cut for scrap by Campbells of Airdrie in January 1968.

John Milton (1608–1674) was an English poet, polemicist, and civil servant for the Commonwealth of England. He is perhaps best known for his epic poem *Paradise Lost*. He perchance deserved his reputation as a polemicist by the virtue of his controversial writings and utterances pertaining mainly to religious subjects. Milton wrote in Latin and Italian as well as English and in doing so gained international acclaim during his lifetime. William Hayley's biography (1796) referred to Milton as the 'greatest English author' and to this day he is regarded as a thinker of worldly importance.

In 1951 Britannia No 70004 was delivered direct to the Festival of Britain exhibition site in London. A special high gloss livery was applied. Note the original style handrails fitted to the smoke deflectors. After the festival, and retaining the special livery, the loco went to the Southern Region where it was initially kept in pristine condition for use on the Golden Arrow boat train service, between London Victoria and Dover Marine for Calais (Maritime) and Paris (Nord). *BR-SR image*

BR Standard Britannia 7MT No 70005 JOHN MILTON, minus nameplates thunders south past Winwick Junction with a fitted freight in September 1966. *Rail Photoprints Collection*

70006 ROBERT BURNS built Crewe Works, entered service April 1951 with a BR1 4250 gallon tender, withdrawn from BR service May 1967. Cut for scrap by McWilliams of Shettleston in October/November 1967.

Robert Burns (1759–1796) (also known as *Rabbie Burns, Scotland's favourite son,* the *Ploughman Poet, Robden of Solway Firth,* the *Bard of Ayrshire* and in Scotland as simply *The Bard*) was a poet and a lyricist. Regarded as the national poet of Scotland his works enjoys worldwide acclaim. In 2009 he was voted by the Scottish public as being the Greatest Scot, through a vote run by Scottish television channel (STV). His poem (and song) *Auld Lang Syne* is often sung at Hogmanay (the last day of the year), and *Scots Wha Hae* served for a long time as an unofficial national anthem of the country.

BR Standard Britannia 7MT No 70006 ROBERT BURNS is pictured at Crewe North (5A) when new and delivered direct from the works. The date was 18 March 1951 a month before the loco entered service. The loco is finished in BR unlined green express passenger livery. Interestingly many pictures examined of new locos in the series 70003 to 70009, and also some later ones (see loco No 70018 section) show that as they were urgently needed they were perchance introduced into traffic 'unlined'. *Michael Bentley Collection*

70007 COEUR-DE-LION built Crewe Works, entered service April 1951 with a BR1 4250 gallon tender, withdrawn from BR service June 1965. Cut for scrap at Crewe Works (BR) in July 1965.

Cœur de Lion, or *Richard the Lionheart,* (1157–1199). Richard I earned his well used epithets even before his accession to the throne, no doubt because of his reputation as a great military leader and warrior. He was King of England from 6 July 1189 until his death. He also ruled as *Duke of Normandy, Duke of Aquitaine, Duke of Gascony, Lord of Cyprus, Count of Anjou, Count of Maine, Count of Nantes, and Overlord of Brittany* at various times during the same period. He actually spent little time in England and in fact spoke only French; between battles he mainly resided at his ancestral home in the Duchy of Aquitaine in the southwest of France.

Britannia Class 7MT No 70007 COEUR-DE-LION is pictured at Crewe North (5A) on 18 March 1951, a month before it officially entered revenue earning service. The engine is in grey primer with smoke box number and nameplates, but no shed plate or cab side number. No 70007 had earlier completed a 'running in' return trip turn to Manchester with a local passenger service. Initially the Britannia class locomotives had small individual foot steps welded to each of the angled uprights below the smokebox door which were later changed to a full step. *Michael Bentley Collection*

Britannia Class 7MT No 70007 COEUR-DE-LION pictured prior to departure at London Liverpool Street station in this 1958 image. *Michael Bentley Collection*

The Pacific (4-6-2) wheel arrangement of the Britannia class is clearly shown in this image of No 70013 OLIVER CROMWELL, taken whilst the loco was sidelined in 2010 for firebox repairs. *Keith Langston*

70008 BLACK PRINCE built Crewe Works, entered service April 1951 with a BR1 4250 gallon tender, withdrawn from BR service January 1967. Cut for scrap by Campbells of Airdrie in May/June 1967.

Black Prince, *Edward of Woodstock, Prince of Wales, Duke of Cornwall, Prince of Aquitaine,* KG (1330–1376) was the eldest son of *King Edward III* of England and *Philippa of Hainault,* and father to *King Richard II* of England. He was an exceptional military leader and his victories over the French first at *Crécy* and then at *Poitiers* made him very popular during his life. In 1348 he became the first Knight of the Garter, an order which he helped to found. Edward died one year before his father, becoming the first English born *Prince of Wales* not to become *King of England.*

BR Standard Britannia 7MT No 70008 BLACK PRINCE restarts a Norwich - Liverpool Street service from its Ipswich stop in late November 1960. John Collins/Rail Photoprints Collection

70009 ALFRED THE GREAT built Crewe Works, entered service May 1951 with a BR1 4250 gallon tender, withdrawn from BR service January 1967. Cut for scrap by McWilliams of Shettleston in May/June 1967.

Alfred the Great (848/849–899) was *King of Wessex* from 871 to 899. Alfred was noted for defending the *Anglo Saxon* regions of southern England against the *Viking* raiders. He is the only *English* monarch to be accorded the epithet 'the Great' and being the first *King of the West Saxons* he styled himself overall *King of the Anglo Saxons*. Himself, a learned man, he encouraged education and improved his

BR Standard Britannia 7MT No 70009 ALFRED THE GREAT stands at Waterloo with the down 'Bournemouth Belle' during the summer of 1951. The 'Bournemouth Belle Pullman Car' was inaugurated in July 1931. The train from London Waterloo to Bournemouth West (until October 1965) and thereafter to Bournemouth Central ran (with a break for WWII) until July 1967 (3 different style headboards were used). *Dave Cobbe Collection – C. R. L. Coles/ Rail Photoprints Collection*

BR Standard Britannia 7MT No 70009 ALFRED THE GREAT was just one month old when this picture was taken at Crewe North (5A) on 30 June 1951, it is carrying a 70A (Nine Elms) shed plate just prior to being delivered to that depot. *Michael Bentley Collection*

kingdom's military structure and legal system. Although never officially canonized he is regarded a *Saint* by some members of the *Catholic* faith whilst the *Anglican Communion* venerates him as a *Christian hero* and afford him a *feast day* on 26th October.

70010 OWEN GLENDOWER built Crewe Works, entered service May 1951 with a BR1 4250 gallon tender, withdrawn from BR service September 1967. Cut for scrap by McWilliams of Shettleston in January 1968.

Owen Glendower (c.1349–c.1416) is *William Shakespeare's* anglicised version of the Welsh name *Owain Glyndŵr* or alternatively *Owain Glyn Dŵr.* He was a Welsh ruler and also the last native Welshman to hold the title *Prince of Wales. Glyndŵr* was a descendant of the *Princes of Powys.* On 16th September 1400 he instigated the Welsh revolt against the English rule of *Henry IV.* Although initially successful, the uprising was eventually put down and *Glyndŵr,* who was last seen publically in 1412, was never captured. Details of the final years of his life still remain a mystery. In 2000, celebrations were held all over Wales to commemorate the 600th anniversary of the *Glyndŵr* rising. In 1966 new name plates were fitted taking into account the Welsh spelling OWAIN GLYNDWR.

BR Standard Britannia 7MT No 70010 OWEN GLENDOWER is seen in the shed yard at Patricroft (then 9H) between duties in this 1965 image. The loco was pictured from the top of the coaling tower. *Jim Carter/Rail Photoprints Collection*

BR Standard Britannia 7MT No 70010 OWEN GLENDOWER waits at Sheffield Victoria in readiness to take over the east bound Manchester–Harwich (Parkeston Quay) while B1 61150 waits in the platform, in this1959 image. *Rail Photoprints Collection*

70011 HOTSPUR built Crewe Works, entered service May 1951 with a BR1 4250 gallon tender, withdrawn from BR service December 1967. Cut for scrap by McWilliams of Shettleston in March/April 1968.

Hotspur is the nickname of *Sir Henry Percy* (1364/66-1404) who was also known as *Harry Hotspur KG* he was the eldest son of Henry Percy, 1st Earl of Northumberland, and 4th Lord Percy of Alnwick. The nickname is suggestive of his impulsive nature. Together with his uncle, *Thomas Percy, Earl of Worcestershire* he led a rebellion against Henry IV in 1403 and formed an alliance with *Owain Glyndŵr*. *Hotspur* met his death during defeat at the *Battle of*

BR Standard Britannia 7MT No 70011 HOTSPUR is seen undergoing its last overhaul in Crewe Works 16 January 1966. Note the 'sustainably built step' on the front buffer beam, a later addition to aid servicing. *Brian Robbins/ Rail Photoprints Collection*

BR Standard Britannia 7MT No 70011 HOTSPUR is seen from the coaling tower in the shed yard Britannia at Patricroft (then 9H) between duties in this 1965 image. *Jim Carter/Rail Photoprints Collection*

Shrewsbury. His remains were first buried at Whitchurch (Salop) but as rumours that he was still alive spread his body was exhumed, cut into quarters, and sent all around England whilst his head was stuck on a pole at the gates of York on the orders of the king.

70012 JOHN OF GAUNT built Crewe Works, entered service May 1951 with a BR1 4250 gallon tender, withdrawn from BR service December 1967. Cut for scrap by Wards of Killamarsh in March/April 1968.

John of Gaunt, 1st Duke of Lancaster KG (1340–1399) was a member of the *House of Plantagenet*, the third surviving son of *King Edward III* of England and *Philippa of Hainault*. He was called *'John of Gaunt'* because he was born in Ghent, Belgium, rendered in English as *Gaunt*. Being the younger brother of *Edward Prince of Wales (The Black Prince)* he was in a good position to exercise great influence over the English throne during the minority of his nephew *Richard II*, and during the ensuing periods of political strife, but was not known as an opponent of the king. He is buried beside his first wife *Blanche of Lancaster* in a magnificent tomb situated in the choir of St. Paul's Cathedral.

BR Standard Britannia 7MT No 70012 JOHN OF GAUNT with northbound freight climbing Grayrigg on 26 August 1967. *David Rostance/Rail Photoprints Collection*

BR Standard Britannia 7MT No 70012 JOHN OF GAUNT pictured at London, Liverpool Street station after arrival from Norwich in this 1960s image. Note the young fireman inside the tender trimming the coal. *Rail Photoprints Collection*

National Collection locomotive No 70013 OLIVER CROMWELL was pictured at Newton Heath depot (9D) just prior to being withdrawn. Note that the nameplates had been removed for safe keeping and that the loco carried a hand painted 12A shed plate (Carlisle). *Keith Langston*

'Running in' turns, new ex works Britannia locomotives were regularly used to haul local return passenger services on the Crewe–Manchester route. (Above) Loco No 70012 JOHN OF GAUNT heads through Wilmslow with a Crewe-Manchester on 25 May 1951. (Below) Loco No 70013 OLIVER CROMWELL is also pictured near Wilmslow with a local service on 31 June 1951. Note that the BR green express passenger livery is lined out in both instances. *Gordon Coltas Trust/Mike Bentley Collection*

70013 OLIVER CROMWELL built Crewe Works, entered service May 1951 with a BR1 4250 gallon tender, withdrawn from BR service August 1968. This locomotive is preserved as part of the National Collection.

Oliver Cromwell (1599–1658) was an English military and political leader who overthrew the English monarchy and temporarily turned England into a republican Commonwealth, he then served as *Lord Protector of England, Scotland and Ireland.* Cromwell was one of the commanders of the *New Model Army* which defeated the royalists in the *English Civil War.* After the execution of *King Charles I* in 1649, Cromwell dominated the short-lived *Commonwealth of England* going on to conquer Ireland and Scotland. He was buried in Westminster Abbey, however after the Royalists returned to power, they had his corpse dug up, hung in chains, and beheaded.

BR Standard Pacific No 70013 OLIVER CROMWELL heads an end of steam railtour on the West Coast Main Line at Moore, south of Warrington, in April 1968. Note that the original nameplates have been removed and replaced by cheap and nasty 'stick on' copies. *Keith Langston*

OLIVER CROMWELL hurries south on the WCML in the early morning mist and through the Cheshire countryside at Moore (between Warrington and Weaver Junction) with a special mixed vehicle postal working in March 1968. Note that the third vehicle in the train is a goods brake van. *Keith Langston*

70014 IRON DUKE built Crewe Works, entered service June 1951 with a BR1 4250 gallon tender, withdrawn from BR service December 1967. Cut for scrap by Wards of Killamarsh in March/April 1968.

Iron Duke *Field Marshal Arthur Wellesley, 1st Duke of Wellington, KG, GCB, GCH, PC, FRS* (1769 –1852), was an Anglo-Irish soldier and statesman. *Wellesley* was born in Ireland where in 1787 he joined the British Army and first served as *aide de camp* to two successive Lord Lieutenants of Ireland. He was also a member of the *Irish House of Commons*. He was a great military leader who ultimately participated in over 60 battles famously defeating *Napoleon* at the Battle of Waterloo. He also served two terms of office as *British Prime Minister* (1828-1830 and 1834) representing the Tory party. Thereafter serving in the *House of Lords* he remained *Commander in Chief of the British Army* until his death.

BR Standard Class 7MT 4-6-2 No 70014 IRON DUKE pictured heading north of Bletchley with a train of non-corridor stock on a Euston–Northampton service in 1964. *David Anderson*

70015 APOLLO built Crewe Works, entered service June 1951 with a BR1 4250 gallon tender, withdrawn from BR service August 1967. Cut for scrap by McWilliams of Shettleston in February 1968.

Apollo was said to be the most widely worshipped of all the *Greek Gods*. *Apollo* was the son of *Zeus* and the *Titan Leto* and was twin brother of *Diana (Artemis)* the goddess of the hunt. He was one of 12 *Olympian Gods* and was also known as *God of the Sun, God of the Arts, God of Medicine, God of Prophecy* and the *protector of herdsmen and their flocks.*

Britannia Class 7MT No 70015 APOLLO is seen minus nameplates on shed at Stockport Edgeley (9B) whilst being serviced in this April 1967 picture. The footplate man shoveling out ash from the smokebox is almost dwarfed by the huge smokebox opening. *Mike Stokes Collection*

Britannia Class 7MT No 70015 APOLLO an ex BR Western Region loco pictured whilst being serviced is seen at Stockport Edgeley (9B), after being re-allocated to BR MR, in this March 1967 image. The smoke deflectors on some BR Western Region allocated Britannia class locos were modified in an attempt to improve the driver's forward vision following a fatal rail crash, that feature can be clearly seen in this image. See the entry for loco No 70026. *Keith Langston*

70016 ARIEL built Crewe Works, entered service June 1951 with a BR1 4250 gallon tender, withdrawn from BR service August 1967. Cut for scrap by McWilliams of Shettleston in December 1967 and January 1968.

Ariel is an archangel associated primarily with *Jewish* and *Christian* mysticism and Apocrypha. Generally presented as an authority over the Earth and its elements, *Ariel* has also been called an angel of healing, wrath and creation. In the Christian Bible's book of *Isaiah*, *Ariel* is a symbolic name for *Jerusalem*. *Ariel* was also a spirit who appeared in *William Shakespeare's* play *The Tempest* and as a 'spirit of the air and chief of the sylphs' in *Alexander Pope's* poem *The Rape of the Lock*.

Britannia Class 7MT No 70016 ARIEL is pictured arriving at Truro on 25 June 1955. *Mike Stokes Collection*

70017 ARROW built Crewe Works, entered service June 1951 with a BR1 4250 gallon tender, withdrawn from BR service September 1966. Cut for scrap by Cashmores of Newport in January/February 1967.

Arrow, straight sharp pointed or metal tipped stick made to be shot from a bow. Perhaps a simplistic choice of name, to travel as swift as an arrow is a commonly used phrase in the English language. Interestingly arrows were very important in Greek mythology as many accounts of the Gods include the carrying or use of bows and arrows.

Britannia Class 7MT No 70017 ARROW pictured during a stop at Earlsfield station (in the south London Borough of Wandsworth) on 26 May 1953. *Roy Vincent/Transport Treasury*

70018 FLYING DUTCHMAN built Crewe Works, entered service June 1951 with a BR1 4250 gallon tender, withdrawn from BR service September 1966. Cut for scrap by Motherwell Machinery & Scrap of Wishaw in May/June 1967.

Flying Dutchman concerns the legend of a ghost ship that can never make port, doomed to sail the oceans forever. The legend is thought to have its origins in 17th century nautical folklore. In 1951 a film entitled *Pandora and the Flying Dutchman* starring *James Mason*, who played sea captain *Hendrick van der Zee* and *Ava Gardner* who played *Pandora,* was released. However in that Hollywood inspired story the *Dutchman* is portrayed as a man and not a ship. The main character was however forced to roam the seas searching for the true meaning of love.

Britannia Class 7MT No 70018 FLYING DUTCHMAN pictured with the up Red Dragon at Pilning in August 1959. 'The Red Dragon' ran between London Paddington and Swansea/Carmarthen from 5 June 1950 until 12 June 1965 (over time four different styles of headboard were carried). *P.M. Alexander/Colour Rail*

BR Standard Britannia 7MT No 70018 FLYING DUTCHMAN is pictured on arrival at London Paddington station with 'The Red Dragon' service in the summer of 1960. Note the BR WR style smoke deflectors with brass lined handholds. *Michael Bentley Collection*

Standard Britannia No 70018 FLYING DUTCHMAN is pictured (above) at Crewe Works when new on 30 June 1951 and (below) in the shed at Crewe North (5A) on 8 May 1963. Note that as new the locomotive was fitted with fluted type coupling and connecting rods in the image above. However over time the driving wheel coupling rods were replaced with tapered rectangular section rods as seen in the image below whilst the profile of the driving rods remained unchanged. *Michael Bentley Collection*

70019 LIGHTNING built Crewe Works, entered service June 1951 with a BR1 4250 gallon tender, withdrawn from BR service March 1966. Cut for scrap by Arnott Young of Troon in June/July 1966.

Lightning is a dramatic atmospheric electrostatic discharge often accompanied by thunder, typically occurring during thunderstorms. During the rapid discharge of atmospheric electricity an associated lightning bolt can travel at speeds in the region of 140,000 mph and reach temperatures of 30,000 degrees centigrade. Ten ships of the *British Royal Navy* have been named *HMS Lightning*.

BR Standard Britannia class Pacific No 70013 OLIVER CROMWELL was pictured at Carnforth depot (10A) prior to working one of several end of steam special charters, the footplate crew are giving the loco a 'last coat of looking over'. *Mike Stokes Collection*

Britannia Class 7MT No 70019 LIGHTNING stands at the platform in Paddington Station on 10 September 1960 with the up 'Red Dragon'. Note BR WR modified smoke deflector hand holds. *D.C. Ovenden/Colour Rail*

Britannia Class 7MT No 70019 LIGHTNING branches off on to the Oxford line connection, from the WCML at Bletchley, with a BR Western Region bound relief express passenger service on 1 August 1964. Note the new catenary posts in position prior to electrification and the grimy condition of the engine which was at that time allocated to Crewe North (5A). *David Anderson*

70020 MERCURY built Crewe Works, entered service July 1951 with a BR1 4250 gallon tender, withdrawn from BR service January 1967. Cut for scrap by McWilliams of Shettleston in May/June 1967.

Mercury was worshiped by Romans as the *God of Travelers*. He was often depicted as a flying warrior with winged hat and sandals and carried winged staffs which were adorned with two intertwined snakes. He was in addition known as the *God of Thieves* as legend tells that when still only a child he stole cattle belonging to the god *Apollo*. Those at British Railways who choose this name for No 70020 would no doubt have preferred *Mercury's* first given calling! Mercury is also one of the planets of our solar system.

Britannia Class 7MT No 70020 MERCURY is turned at York Depot in preparation for heading the return Home Counties Railway Society special back to London Kings Cross on 4 October 1964. *Rail Photoprints Collection*

70021 MORNING STAR built Crewe Works, entered service August 1951 with a BR1 4250 gallon tender, withdrawn from BR service December 1967. Cut for scrap by Wards of Inverkeithing in April/ May 1968.

Morning Star is the name given to the planet Venus by virtue of the fact that it appears in the east before sunrise. The planet is named after *Venus* the *Roman* goddess of love and beauty. *Venus* reaches its maximum brightness shortly before sunrise or shortly after sunset, for which reason it has been known as either/or the *Morning Star* or the *Evening Star*. (See loco 70023 *Venus*)

A wonderful image from a long lost but not forgotten picturesque railway route, Britannia Class 7MT No 70021 MORNING STAR is pictured passing Millers Dale Signal Box on the former Midland main line (now a walking route) with an up Manchester – St. Pancras express in 1960. *Alan H. Bryant ARPS/Rail Photoprints Collection*

70022 TORNADO built Crewe Works, entered service August 1951 with a BR1 4250 gallon tender, withdrawn from BR service December 1967. Cut for scrap by Wards of Inverkeithing in March/April 1968.

Tornado is a highly dangerous rotating column of air that is in contact with the earth and a cloud formation at the same time. Tornadoes form in varied shapes and sizes but are typically visible in the form of a funnel whose narrow end (spout) touches the earth and is often encircled by a dust cloud.

Britannia Class 7MT No 70022 TORNADO in a very clean condition and hauling BR WR red and cream stock is pictured leaving Abelton Lane Tunnel, near Severn Tunnel Junction with an up train in this 1958 image. *P.M. Alexander/Colour Rail*

70023 VENUS built Crewe Works, entered service August 1951 with a BR1 4250 gallon tender, withdrawn from BR service December 1967. Cut for scrap by Wards of Killamarsh in April 1968.

Venus is a *Roman Goddess* who is associated with love, beauty and fertility; she played an important part in many *Roman* religious festivals and her name is associated with many myths. Venus is also the name given to the easiest star to see with the naked eye shining as it does with a brilliant white light. (See loco 70021 *Morning Star*

Britannia Class 7MT No 70023 VENUS heads south from Lancaster with an up parcels train, July 1963. *Dave Cobbe/Rail Photoprints Collection*

Britannia Class 7MT No 70023 VENUS pictured in May 1958 hauling the up 'Capitals United Express' at Tyford BR WR. 'The Capitals United Express' ran between London Paddington and Cardiff/Swansea High Street in the period February 1956 to June 1965, 4 styles of headboard were used. The BR WR brass edged smoke deflector handholds are clearly visible in this classic WR image. *T.B. Owen/Colour Rail*

70024 VULCAN built Crewe Works, entered service August 1951 with a BR1 4250 gallon tender, withdrawn from BR service December 1967. Cut for scrap by Wards of Killamarsh in April 1968.

Vulcan according to *Roman* mythology was the son of *Jupiter*, the king of the gods for whom he made thunderbolts and *Juno* the queen of the gods. He was considered to be the maker of arms, iron, jewelry and items of armor for many of the other gods. His smithy was said to be situated beneath the Volcano *Mount Etna* in Sicily.

Britannia Class 7MT No 70024 VULCAN, pictured at the famous ex GWR motive power depot of Old Oak Common (81A) on 8 May 1955. *A.E. Bennet/Transport Treasury*

Britannia Class 7MT No 70024 VULCAN storms away from Reading with a BR WR Paddington-Pembroke Dock service, although the image is dated post Milton accident (see entry for loco No 70026) the loco still carries original smoke box handrails, May 1958. *W.Oliver/Colour Rail*

70025 WESTERN STAR built Crewe Works, entered service September 1952 with a BR1A 5000 gallon tender, withdrawn from BR service December 1967. Cut for scrap by Campbells of Airdrie in January 1968.

Western Star was a name originally used by the *Great Western Railway* (GWR) for a locomotive of the *Star Class* and the name reflected that railway company's geographical westerly direction. The title '*Western Star*' refers to no particular star.

Britannia Class 7MT No 70025 WESTERN STAR is pictured at Carlisle in September 1967. The loco is preparing to leave the train having worked in with the 3.15pm Crewe-Carlisle service. Note the young enthusiasts; Carlisle was a great place to see Britannia Class Pacific class locos towards the end of the steam era. *Roger Jermy*

Britannia Class 7MT No 70025 WESTERN STAR prepares to leave the shed yard at shed at Patricroft (then 9H) having been coaled and watered, in May 1964. Note the coaling plant behind the loco and also the fireman on the tender having just taken out 'the bag'. *Jim Carter/Rail Photoprints Collection*

70026 POLAR STAR built Crewe Works, entered service October 1952 with a BR1A 5000 gallon tender, withdrawn from BR service December 1967. Cut for scrap by Cashmores of Newport in April/May 1967.

Polar Star was a previously used *Great Western Railway* (GWR) locomotive name. A *Polar Star* was of great importance to early navigators in that it appears fixed and unmoving over the earth's North or South Pole. However the only one visible to the naked eye is *Polaris (aka The Pole Star or North Star)*. No 70026 was involved in a fatal railcrash which claimed the lives of eleven persons and caused injury to almost 150 others. After the findings of an enquiry into the accident the BR WR modified the smokebox handrails on their allocation of Britannia 7MT locos as impaired forward vision was said to be a contributory factor, the loco was repaired and returned to traffic after repair.

The crash occurred at about 13:15 on Sunday 20 November 1955, at Milton, between Steventon and Didcot on the line from Swindon. The train involved was the 08:30 excursion train from Treherbert, South Wales, consisting of ten coaches hauled by Britannia Pacific No 70026 Polar Star. The train failed to slow down for a low speed crossover. The engine and several carriages rolled down an embankment, which added to the severity of the accident.

Britannia Class 7MT No 70026 POLAR STAR provides power to spare. This short train pictured near Chippenham was a regular evening 'running in ' turn from Swindon Works, a 1954 image. *Rail Photoprints Collection*

70027 RISING STAR built Crewe Works, entered service October 1952 with a BR1A 5000 gallon tender, withdrawn from BR service June 1967. Cut for scrap by Motherwell Machinery & Scrap of Wishaw in November 1967.

Rising Star was a previously used *Great Western Railway* (GWR) locomotive name. The name was chosen to represent that company's perceived status. *Rising Star* is a commonly used term to indicate metaphorically that a person's standing or reputation is rapidly increasing.

Britannia Class 7MT No 70027 RISING STAR is pictured near Hayes & Harlington with the up 'Red Dragon' July 1956. *Rail Photoprints Collection*

70028 ROYAL STAR built Crewe Works, entered service October 1952 with a BR1A 5000 gallon tender, withdrawn from BR service September 1967. Cut for scrap by McWilliams of Shettleston in January/February 1968.

Royal Star was a previously used *Great Western Railway* (GWR) locomotive name. The four *Persian 'royal stars'* are *Aldebaran, Regulus, Antares* and *Fomalhaut*, which are said to guard the four quarters of the annual night sky.

Britannia Class 7MT No 70028 ROYAL STAR hurries through Tring on 28 July 1962 with a down relief express service. Whilst the railway man on the up platform shows no interest in the train the young enthusiasts on the wall of the down platform certainly do! *Ron Smith/Transport Treasury*

70029 SHOOTING STAR built Crewe Works, entered service November 1952 with a BR1A 5000 gallon tender, withdrawn from BR service October 1967. Cut for scrap by McWilliams of Shettleston in February 1968.

Shooting Star was a previously used *Great Western Railway* (GWR) locomotive name. It is the common term used to describe a meteor.

Britannia Class 7MT No 70029 SHOOTING STAR at Paddington with a down express, pictured in 1957. *Rail Photoprints Collection*

Britannia Class 7MT No 70029 SHOOTING STAR pictured in 1958 when 'on shed' at Shrewsbury (89A). *Rail Photoprints Collection*

70030 WILLIAM WORDSWORTH built Crewe Works, entered service November 1952 with a BR1 4250 gallon tender, withdrawn from BR service May 1966. Cut for scrap by Wards of Beighton in October 1966.

William Wordsworth (1770–1850) was a major English romantic poet. He was born in an impressive Georgian house in Cockermouth, Cumbria, which stands to this day and is now called *Wordsworth House*. He is universally remembered for the poem *'I Wandered Lonely as a Cloud'* which is more commonly referred to as *'Daffodils' written* in 1804 and first published in 1807. He was appointed by the then Prime Minister, *Sir Robert Peel* to the post of *Poet Laureate* in 1843 a role he held until his death.

Britannia Class 7MT No 70030 WILLIAM WORDSWORTH pictured at Willesden shed on 8 November 1964. The locomotive is seen in filthy exterior condition, although still with nameplates attached. Loco cleaning at '1A' had obviously come to an end at that time! However No 70030 was to serve a further 18 months in traffic before being withdrawn. *Rail Photoprints Collection*

70031 BYRON built Crewe Works, entered service November 1952 with a BR1 4250 gallon tender, withdrawn from BR service November 1967. Cut for scrap by McWilliams of Shettleston in March 1968.

Byron, *George Gordon Byron, 6th Baron Byron*, later *George Gordon Noel, 6th Baron Byron, FRS* (1788 – 1824), commonly known simply as *Lord Byron*, was an English poet and a leading figure in the *Romantic Movement*. His name was however synonymous with aristocratic excesses which included huge debt, a multiplicity of love affairs and even one scandalous incestuous dalliance with his half sister. Byron was famously described by *Lady Caroline Lamb* (a married lady with whom he had an affair) as being collectively 'mad, bad and dangerous to know'.

Britannia Class 7MT No 70031 BYRON is pictured north of Bletchley on the WCML with an up relief express in this 1960 image. *David Anderson*

70032 TENNYSON built Crewe Works, entered service November 1952 with a BR1 4250 gallon tender, withdrawn from BR service September 1967. Cut for scrap by McWilliams of Shettleston in February/March 1968.

Tennyson, *Alfred Tennyson, Ist Baron Tennyson, Alfred Lord Tennyson FRS* (1809-1892) was *Poet Laureate* during much of *Queen Victoria's* reign and he remains to this day one of the most popular poets in the English language. He was a prolific author who excelled at writing short lyrics. *Tennyson* was responsible for penning a great many phrases which having endured the test of time are still used in the present day for example *'Theirs not to reason why – Theirs but to do and die'*.

Britannia Class 7MT No 70032 TENNYSON, seen here minus nameplates and smokebox number plate, prepares to leave Preston with a southbound express in September 1966. *Roger Jermy*

70033 CHARLES DICKENS built Crewe Works, entered service December 1952 with a BR1 4250 gallon tender, withdrawn from BR service July 1967. Cut for scrap by Campbells of Airdrie in April/May 1968.

Charles Dickens, *Charles John Huffam Dickens* (1812–1870) was an English novelist of great importance. He achieved great fame during his lifetime when he was considered by many to be the finest writer of the *Victorian* period. The enduring popularity of his novels has ensured that some have never actually gone out of print. He was born in Landport Hampshire to John and Elizabeth Dickens and he was the second born of their eight children. Readers will be familiar with his works and the story lines of *'A Christmas Carol'* and perchance *'Oliver Twist'* will readily come to mind.

Britannia Class 7MT No 70033 CHARLES DICKENS is minus nameplates and displaying a chalked on '5B' shed plate (Crewe South) but surprisingly still retains what looks like a genuine BR smokebox number plate, pictured on the Didcot East avoiding line in March 1967. *David Anderson*

70034 THOMAS HARDY built Crewe Works, entered service December 1952 with a BR1 4250 gallon tender, withdrawn from BR service July 1967. Cut for scrap by McWilliams of Shettleston in September/October 1967.

Thomas Hardy OM (1840–1928) was an English novelist and poet. Hardy regarded himself firstly as a poet and maintained that he wrote novels 'only for financial gain'. His novels are however perhaps what he is best remembered for. Much of his fictional works were set in the semi-fictional region of *Wessex* and in the main his writings explored the lives of characters struggling to come to terms with their social circumstances. *Tess of the d'Urbervilles* and *Far from the Madding Crowd* are two of his better known novels. He was born in Stinsford, Dorchester, Dorset to stonemason Thomas Hardy and his wife Jemima.

Britannia Class 7MT No 70034 THOMAS HARDY, seen shunting ash/coal wagons at Bath Green Park, Somerset and Dorset Joint Railway on 1 May 1965. The visit is thought by the photographer to be the only one ever made to that depot by a Britannia class locomotive. *John Chalcraft/Rail Photoprints Collection*

Britannia Class 7MT No 70034 THOMAS HARDY being serviced at Crewe South (5B) in 1963. *Rail Photoprints Collection*

70035 RUDYARD KIPLING built Crewe Works, entered service December 1952 with a BR1 4250 gallon tender, withdrawn from BR service December 1967. Cut for scrap by Wards of Inverkeithing in March/April 1968.

Rudyard Kipling, *Joseph Rudyard Kipling* (1865–1936) was an English novelist and short story writer who is perhaps mainly remembered for his tales and poems of British soldiers in *India,* and his tales especially written for the enjoyment of children. Born in Bombay, India to English parents John and Alice Kipling he was given the name *Rudyard* because his parents had courted at *Rudyard Lake* in Staffordshire. *Kipling* was the recipient of the *1907 Nobel Prize for Literature.* His many popular works include *The Jungle Book (1894)* and The Man Who Would Be King (1888). Kipling reportedly declined both the opportunity to be Poet Laureate and a knighthood.

Britannia Class 7MT No 70035 RUDYARD KIPLING gets smartly away from Leeds with short parcels train, the loco is minus nameplates in this winter 1966 image. *Mike Stokes Collection*

70036 BOADICEA built Crewe Works, entered service December 1952 with a BR1 4250 gallon tender, withdrawn from BR service October 1966. Cut for scrap by Motherwell Machinery & Scrap of Wishaw in February 1967.

Boadicea, also known as *Boudicca* (AD60-61) was the Queen of the British *Iceni Tribe* who famously led an uprising against the occupying troops of the *Roman Empire.* The historic events of that time were revived during the *Victorian* era and that led to an increase in the warrior Queen's legendary fame with *Queen Victoria* being fancifully portrayed as her namesake. *Boadicea (Boudicca)* has ever since remained a cultural symbol in the UK.

Britannia Class 7MT No 70036 BOADICEA is in a filthy exterior condition and minus nameplates, pictured heading south past Weaver Junction with an up freight, circa 1965. *Colin Whitfield/Rail Photoprints Collection*

Britannia Class 7MT No 70036 BOADICEA on shed at Stratford (30A), circa 1956. *Rail Photoprints Collection*

BR Standard 'Britannia' class Pacific No 70037 HEREWARD THE WAKE was pictured when spotlessly turned out by Stratford depot, No 70037 prepares to head out of London Liverpool Street station with the Railway Correspondents Travel Society (RCTS London Branch) 'Fensman' special train, 24 July 1955. *Hugh Ballantyne/Rail Photoprints Collection*

70037 HEREWARD THE WAKE built Crewe Works, entered service December 1952 with a BR1 4250 gallon tender, withdrawn from BR service October 1966. Cut for scrap by McWilliams of Airdrie in February 1968.

Hereward the Wake, who came to be remembered as an English hero, hailed from Bourne in Lincolnshire and was of *Danish* ancestry. Living during Saxon times his birth and death dates are uncertain, however he was by all accounts a willful young man whom *King Edward the Confessor* saw fit to exile to Europe at the age of 14. *Hereward* returned to Britain after the defeat of *King Harold* and he set about exacting revenge on as many *Normans* as he could. *Charles Kingsley* in his novel *Hereward* (1865) portrayed him as the son of *Leofric Earl of Mercia.*

Britannia Class 7MT No 70037 HEREWARD THE WAKE is seen under the train shed roof at Huddersfield, circa 1960. *Rail Photoprints Collection*

Britannia Class 7MT No 70037 HEREWARD THE WAKE in extremely clean exterior condition is seen between turns 'on shed' at Stratford (30A) in 1956. *Rail Photoprints Collection*

70038 ROBIN HOOD built Crewe Works, entered service January 1953 with a BR1 4250 gallon tender, withdrawn from BR service August 1967. Cut for scrap by McWilliams of Shettleston in January/February 1968.

Robin Hood was an outlaw famously portrayed in English folklore, he was by all accounts a highly skilled archer and swordsman who gained popularity amongst the hard pressed common people in *Medieval Times* by reputedly robbing the rich only to give to the poor. With his intrepid band supporters, known as the *Merry Men* he was said to be based beyond harm's way deep within *Sherwood Forest* from where he waged a protracted war like feud with his adversary the *Sheriff of Nottingham.*

Britannia Class 7MT No 70038 ROBIN HOOD, then a Kingmoor allocated Britannia is pictured at Patricroft, circa 1965. Note that the original nameplates and smokebox number plates have been replaced with imitations. *Jim Carter/Rail Photoprints Collection*

70039 SIR CHRISTOPHER WREN built Crewe Works, entered service February 1953 with a BR1 4250 gallon tender, withdrawn from BR service September 1967. Cut for scrap by McWilliams of Shettleston in January/February 1968.

Sir Christopher Wren FRS (1632–1723) was one of the most highly acclaimed English architects; he was also an accomplished astronomer. After the *Great Fire of London* (1666) he played a big part in the rebuilding of the city. His world famous masterpiece is *St. Paul's Cathedral* and other notable buildings by *Wren* include the *Royal Naval College* in Greenwich and the south front of *Hampton Court Palace*. The son of a Rector he was born in East Knowle, Wiltshire.

Britannia Class 7MT No 70039 SIR CHRISTOPHER WREN, when an Immingham (40B) allocated loco, passes Brookmans Park with a Cleethorpes - Kings Cross service on 6 May 1962. *Rail Photoprints Collection*

70040 CLIVE OF INDIA built Crewe Works, entered service March 1953 with a BR1 4250 gallon tender, withdrawn from BR service September 1967. Cut for scrap by McWilliams of Shettleston in November/December 1967.

Clive of India, *Major-General Robert Clive, 1st Baron Clive, KB* (1725 – 1774), was a British army officer who became *British Governor of Bengal.* He is credited with establishing the *East India Company* in Bengal and together with *Warren Hastings* being a key figure in the creation of *British India.* Not bad for a Shropshire born lad who was expelled from three different schools! He was the eldest son of 13 children. There is an impressive monument to *Clive* on King Charles Street London.

Britannia Class 7MT No 70040 CLIVE OF INDIA pictured 'on shed'at Patricroft in March 1965. *Jim Carter/Rail Photoprints Collection*

Britannia Class 7MT No 70040 CLIVE OF INDIA pictured at Crewe Works during what must have been the loco's final overhaul on 16 January 1965. *Brian Robbins/Rail Photoprints Collection*

70041 SIR JOHN MOORE built Crewe Works, entered service March 1953 with a BR1 4250 gallon tender, withdrawn from BR service April 1967. Cut for scrap by McWilliams of Shettleston in September/October 1967.

Sir John Moore, *Lieutenant-General Sir John Moore, KB* (1761–1809) was a celebrated British soldier who also served as a *Member of Parliament.* He is remembered for his participation in many military campaigns, for his introduction of military training reforms and for initiating the construction of the *Martello Towers* on the south coast of England. He was killed during the *Battle of Corunna* during the *Peninsular War* and his tomb is situated in *San Carlos Garden* at *A Coruña.* Moore was born in Glasgow where his father (also John Moore) was an eminent doctor and writer. A bronze statue in the form of a monument to him stands in the city of his birth.

Although undated this 1950's picture of Britannia Class 7MT No 70041 SIR JOHN MOORE making a spirited departure from Lowestoft certainly has its origins in winter as melting snow is to be seen on the ground and even on the roofs of the first two carriages. *Dr Ian C. Allen/Transport Treasury*

Britannia Class 7MT No 70041 SIR JOHN MOORE pictured southbound at speed near Winwick Junction WCML, in February 1964. *Jim Carter/ Rail Photoprints Collection*

70042 LORD ROBERTS built Crewe Works, entered service April 1953 with a BR1 4250 gallon tender, withdrawn from BR service May 1967. Cut for scrap by McWilliams of Shettleston in November/December 1967.

Lord Roberts, *Field Marshal Frederick Sleigh Roberts, 1st Earl Roberts, Bt, VC, KG, KP, GCB, OM, GCSI, GCIE, KStJ, PC* (1832 –1914) was a distinguished and highly decorated British soldier who was without doubt one of the most successful British commanders of the 19th century. He was born in India and was the second son of Irish born *General Sir Abraham Roberts* and Edinburgh born Isabella Bunbury. *Lord Roberts* died of pneumonia whilst visiting WWI troops in France. He was only one of two non-royals to be afforded the privilege of *lying in state* prior to a state funeral in *St. Paul's Cathedral* during the 20th century, the other being *Sir Winston Churchill.* Lord Roberts rests within St. Paul's and there is a monument to him in Glasgow.

Britannia Class 7MT No 70042 LORD ROBERTS pictured hauling an up Midland Express at an unknown location during 1960. *Alan H. Bryant ARPS/ Rail Photoprints Collection*

70043 LORD KITCHENER built Crewe Works, entered service June 1953 with a BR1 4250 gallon tender, withdrawn from BR service August 1965. Cut for scrap by Wards of Beighton in October/November 1965.

Lord Kitchener, *Field Marshall Horatio Herbert Kitchener, 1st Earl Kitchener KG, KP, GCB, OM, GCSI, GCMG, GCIE, ADC, PC* (1850-1916) was an Irish born highly decorated British soldier who also served in the Cabinet as *Secretary of State for War (1914).* His commanding image is remembered to this day from the *First World War* recruiting poster stating *'Your country needs you!'* In 1898 he won fame for securing victory at *The Battle of Omdurman* in the Sudan, after which he was given the title *Lord Kitchener of Khartoum. Kitchener* was born in Ballylongford County Kerry, son of Lt. Col. Henry Horatio Kitchener and Frances Anne Chevallier-Cole. He died in 1916 when the warship taking him to negotiations in Russia was sunk by a German mine near the Orkney Islands.

Britannia Class 7MT No 70043 LORD KITCHENER pictured travelling northbound on WCML at Dutton Viaduct, September 1962. *R. A. Whitfield/ Rail Photoprints Collection*

70044 EARL HAIG built Crewe Works, entered service June 1954 with a BR1 4250 gallon tender, withdrawn from BR service December 1966. Cut for scrap by Wards of Beighton in February 1967.

Earl Haig, Douglas Haig, 1st Earl Haig, KT, GCB, OM, GCVO, KCIE, ADC, (1861–1928) was a senior British Army officer during World War 1. Haig was commander of the *British Expeditionary Force (BEF)* from 1915 until the end of the war. He was commander during the *Battle of the Somme* where the British Army suffered the highest number of battle causalities ever in military history. Haig went on to command the army during the *Third Battle of Ypres* and the *Hundred Days Offensive* which followed. He was born in Edinburgh and his father John Haig, was head of the family whisky distilling business Haig & Haig.

Britannia Class 7MT No 70044 EARL HAIG leaves Manchester London Road with the up 'Mancunian' for Euston, 1959. 'The Mancunian' ran between London Euston and Manchester London Road from September 1927 until September 1960 when the service then transferred to Manchester Piccadilly. No headboard was carried between 1939 and 1949. *Rail Photoprints Collection*

Britannia Class 7MT No 70044 EARL HAIG pictured at speed with an up express near Winsford on the WCML in August 1963. *R. A. Whitfield/ Rail Photoprints Collection*

70045 LORD ROWALLAN built Crewe Works, entered service June 1954 with a BR1D 4725 gallon tender with steam powered coal pusher, withdrawn from BR service December 1967. Cut for scrap by Wards of Beighton in February/March 1968.

Lord Rowallan, Thomas Godfrey Olson Corbett, 2nd Baron Rowallan, KT, KBE, MC, TD (1895–1977) was a senior British Army officer. He served with distinction in both wars (1914–1918 and 1939–1945). In 1939 he raised a new *Territorial Army* battalion of the *Royal Scots Fusiliers* with whom he served with in France as part of the *British Expeditionary Force (BEF).* On being demobilized from the army he took up the post of *Chief Scout of the British Commonwealth and Empire* and also served for a period as *Governor of Tasmania* He was the first son of property developer, and Liberal Politician Archibald Corbett and Alice Mary Polson, born in Chelsea he died at Rowallan Castle Kilmarnock.

Britannia Class 7MT No 70045 LORD ROWALLAN prepares to leave Bristol Temple Meads with a summer Saturday service for the Midlands pictured on 3 July 1965. No70045 was in 1967 fitted with LMS-style oval buffers in the course of repairs after minor collision damage. *John Chalcraft/Rail Photoprints Collection*

Britannia Class 7MT No 70045 LORD ROWALLAN pictured 'on shed' at Carlisle Upperby (12B) in 1962. *Rail Photoprints Collection*

70046 ANZAC built Crewe Works, entered service June 1954 with a BR1D 4725 gallon tender with steam powered coal pusher, withdrawn from BR service July 1967. Cut for scrap by Campbells of Airdrie in December 1967/ January 1968.

Anzac, the Australian and New Zealand Army Corps. Initially this acronym was used to describe a First World War *Mediterranean Expeditionary Force* that was formed in Egypt during 1915, and which fought with great distinction during the *Battle of Gallipoli.* The corps was officially disbanded in 1916 following the allied evacuation of the Gallipoli peninsular and the subsequent formation of the 1st and 2nd Anzac Corps. Over time Anzac became the term used to describe any military formation containing Australian or New Zealand units. *Anzac Day* is a national day of remembrance in Australia and New Zealand, commemorated annually on 25 April.

Britannia Class 7MT No 70046 ANZAC pictured 'on shed' at Willesden (1A) on 11 August 1963 is in a reasonable exterior condition but is minus nameplates. *Rail Photoprints Collection*

70047 built Crewe Works, entered service June 1954 with a BR1D 4725 gallon tender with steam powered coal pusher, withdrawn from BR service July 1967. Cut for scrap by Campbells of Airdrie in December 1967. This locomotive was the only member of the class never to be accorded a name.

Britannia Class 7MT No 70047, the un-named member of the class is pictured at Chester, whilst backing onto a southbound train in June 1964. *Jim Carter/Rail Photoprints Collection*

70048 THE TERRITORIAL ARMY 1908–1958, built Crewe Works, entered service July 1954 with a BR1D 4725 gallon tender with steam powered coal pusher, withdrawn from BR service May 1967. Cut for scrap by McWilliams of Shettleston in September/October 1967.

The Territorial Army 1908–1958, originally entered BR service unnamed, being subsequently named on 23rd July 1958. The Territorial Army, or TA as it is commonly referred to, is part of the UK's reserve land forces, which provides support to the regular army at home and overseas. The TA is the largest of all the countries reserve forces.

Britannia Class 7MT No 70048 THE TERRITORIAL ARMY 1908-1958 pictured at Stockport with a Manchester bound freight, circa 1960. *Rail Photoprints Collection*

70049 SOLWAY FIRTH, built Crewe Works, entered service July 1954 with a BR1D 4725 gallon tender with steam powered coal pusher, withdrawn from BR service December 1967. Cut for scrap by McWilliams of Shettleston in March 1968.

Solway Firth, Scotland is a firth (estuary) that forms part of the border between England and Scotland, between Cumbria (including the Solway Plain) and Dumfries and Galloway. It stretches from St Bees Head, just south of Whitehaven in Cumbria, to the Mull of Galloway, on the western end of Dumfries and Galloway. The Isle of Man is also very near to the firth. The firth comprises part of the Irish Sea.

Britannia Class 7MT No 70049 SOLWAY FIRTH is pictured 'on shed' at Holyhead (6J) prior to joining its southbound train, the loco carries The 'Irish Mail' headboard. The 'Irish Mail' headboard was officially carried on 26th September 1927 however the London Euston-Holyhead boat train service had been referred to as the 'Irish Mail' since 1848 making it the earliest known 'title' of any train in the UK. After a break during WWII the headboard was re-introduced on 31 May 1948 and the famous service last ran (electric traction hauled Euston-Crewe-Euston and diesel hauled Crewe –Holyhead-Crewe) on 12 May 1985. Keith Langston

70050 FIRTH OF CLYDE, built Crewe Works, entered service August 1954 with a BR1D 4725 gallon tender with steam powered coal pusher, withdrawn from BR service December 1966. Cut for scrap by Campbells of Airdrie in November/December 1966.

Firth of Clyde, Scotland forms a large area of coastal water, sheltered from the Atlantic Ocean by the Kintyre Peninsula which encloses the outer firth in Argyll and Ayrshire, Scotland. The Kilbrannan Sound is a large arm of the Firth of Clyde, separating the Kintyre Peninsula from the Isle of Arran.

Britannia Class 7MT No 70050 FIRTH OF CLYDE pictured hard at work on Beattock Bank (WCML) with the 9.30am Manchester Victoria to Glasgow Central express, July 1958. *David Anderson*

70051 FIRTH OF FORTH, built Crewe Works, entered service August 1954 with a BR1D 4725 gallon tender with steam powered coal pusher, withdrawn from BR service December 1967. Cut for scrap by McWilliams of Shettleston in March 1968.

Firth of Forth Scotland, the firth, which was known as *Bodotria* in Roman times is the estuary of the River Forth. The river flows into the North Sea between Fife to the north and West Lothian, the city of Edinburgh and East Lothian to the south. Geologically speaking the Firth of Forth is a *fjord* formed by the *Forth Glacier*. The famous Forth Railway Bridge (1.5 miles long) is of special interest to railway enthusiasts.

Britannia Class 7MT No 70051 FIRTH OF FORTH is pictured being turned on the Patricroft turntable in April 1963. *Jim Carter/Rail Photoprints Collection*

70052 FIRTH OF TAY, built Crewe Works, entered service August 1954 with a BR1D 4725 gallon tender with steam powered coal pusher, withdrawn from BR service April 1967. Cut for scrap by Campbells of Airdrie in October 1967.

Firth of Tay Scotland, which flows into the North Sea, is situated between the areas known as Fife, Perth & Kinross, the city of Dundee and Angus. The River Tay, which empties into the firth, has the largest rate of flow of any Scottish river. The firth is crossed by an impressive 2.25 mile long rail bridge completed in 1887 (the Second Tay Bridge) which replaced the original rail bridge destroyed during a fierce storm in 1879 with the tragic loss of 79 lives.

Britannia Class 7MT No 70052 FIRTH OF TAY pictured in action with a down fast fitted freight, despite carrying an express passenger lamp code the train had been halted by signals at Carstairs Junction, in 1964. *David Anderson*

Loco No 70052 was involved in a serious accident at Blea Moor on 21 January 1960, when working an overnight sleeper train from Glasgow to Leeds which resulted in 5 fatalities. The accident investigators found that the Britannia Pacific had suffered the collapse of its 'crosshead' which in turn led to the failure of it's 'motion' which when torn free of the loco collided with a passing freight train. The train engine of the freight was derailed towards No 70052's train and tore out the sides of three passenger coaches. The root cause was said to be a failure to tighten slide bar nuts; a problem which had been reported several times previously but without fatal consequences. As a result of the enquiry the difficult to access nuts were redesigned.

Britannia Class 7MT No 70052 FIRTH OF TAY in BR plain green livery (with red background to the name plate) is seen at Nottingham Midland station in April 1964. *Colour Rail*

70053 MORAY FIRTH, built Crewe Works, entered service September 1954 with a BR1D 4725 gallon tender with steam powered coal pusher, withdrawn from BR service April 1967. Cut for scrap by McWilliams of Shettleston in September/October 1967.

Moray Firth Scotland is fed by a number of rivers which include the River Ness, the River Findhorn and the River Spey, the firth empties into the North Sea it is easily Scotland's largest firth. The roughly triangular body of water is situated north and east of Inverness. The Moray Firth is effectively two firths, the Inner Moray Firth (also known as the Firth of Inverness) and the Outer Moray Firth.

Britannia Class 7MT No 70053 MORAY FIRTH heads a southbound express service away from Leeds. Note that the loco is fitted with a later design of BR MR smoke deflectors without handrails and is minus its nameplates, in this April 1967 picture. *Mike Stokes Collection*

70054 DORNOCH FIRTH, built Crewe Works, entered service September 1954 with a BR1D 4725 gallon tender with steam powered coal pusher, withdrawn from BR service November 1966. Cut for scrap by Motherwell Machinery & Scrap of Wishaw in May/June 1967.

Dornoch Firth Scotland, which empties into the North Sea, is situated on the east coast of the Highland Region in Northern Scotland, and that body of water forms part of the boundary between Ross and Cromarty to the south and Sutherland to the north. Together with *Loch Fleet* it is designated as a Special Protection Area (SPA).

Britannia Class 7MT No 70054 DORNOCH FIRTH leaves Leeds City with the down 'Thames-Clyde Express', circa 1960, no headboard is carried in this image. The 'Thames Clyde Express' ran between London St, Pancras and Glasgow St. Enoch between September 1927 until June 1966 when St. Enoch station closed and the train was redirected to Glasgow Central. With a ten year break during WWII the service ran until 3 May 1975. *Jim Carter/Rail Photoprints Collection*

On 8 November 2008 preserved sister loco No. 70013 (BR standard class 7 70013 Oliver Cromwell) was temporarily re-numbered as 70048, and carried the original 'Territorial Army 1908 - 1958' nameplate (red back ground) on the right hand side smoke deflector. This was carried out as part of a ceremony to temporarily re-name the loco as part of the 100th anniversary of the Territorial Army. The new name was carried on the left hand side smoke deflector, and naming was performed by HRH The Duke of Gloucester at Quorn station on the preserved Great Central Railway. *Fred Kerr*

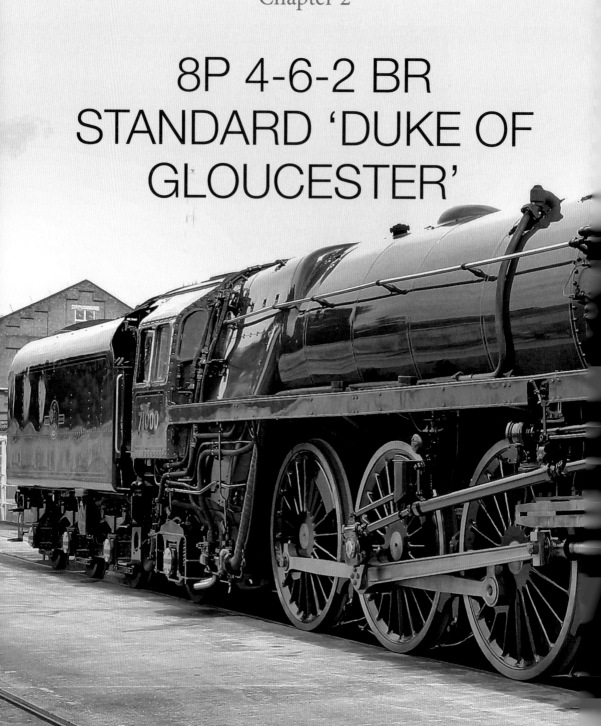

Chapter 2

8P 4-6-2 BR STANDARD 'DUKE OF GLOUCESTER'

A magnificent sight, restored Standard 8P Pacific No 71000 DUKE OF GLOUCESTER visited Crewe Works in July 2004 in order to receive a new livery. The locomotive is pictured adjacent to the erecting shop in which 'she' was built in 1954. *Keith Langston*

71000 DUKE OF GLOUCESTER built Crewe Works, entered service May 1954 with a BR1E 4725 gallon tender, changed to a new BR1J 4325 gallon tender in 1957. No 71000 was the last express passenger steam locomotive to be built in the UK. Withdrawn from BR service in November 1962, this locomotive is preserved and is in private ownership.

The Prince Henry, Duke of Gloucester (Henry William Frederick Albert (1900–1974) a member of the *British Royal Family*, the third son of George V of the United Kingdom and Queen Mary, and was therefore uncle to *Queen Elizabeth II*. The Duke served as a soldier for most of his life and was also the 11th Governor-General of Australia (1945 to 1947). Current Duke (2012) Prince Richard, Duke of Gloucester (Richard Alexander Walter George; born 26 August 1944) Prince Richard is the youngest grandchild of King George V and Queen Mary. He has been Duke of Gloucester since his father's death in 1974 and is currently 20th in the line of succession. The Duke supported the restoration of the locomotive which bears his title and he has enjoyed a close association with No 71000 and he is Honorary President of 'The 71000 (Duke of Gloucester) Steam Locomotive Trust'.

BR Standard 8P Pacific

During the planning stages of the new BR Standard locomotive range designs provision was made to include a large express passenger Pacific design, although at that time BR did not anticipate an immediate need for such a class of locomotives. This 'would be' new Pacific design was expected to be nothing more than a modified Stanier 'Duchess' class 4-6-2 with four cylinders, double blastpipe and chimney and bar frames.

Those BR bosses who were expecting a modified Duchess type 4-6-2 with four cylinders were in for a shock as the resultant replacement locomotive for No 46202 followed anything but those design criteria. The new Pacific emerged from the works as a three cylinder locomotive which was itself a departure from BR Standard practice that hitherto had employed only two cylinder designs on the smaller Class 6 (Clan) and 7 (Britannia) Pacific engines. Perhaps the most striking difference to the lineside observer was the addition of British Caprotti rotary cam poppet valve gear to the cylinders, driven by shafts attached to the centre driving wheels and easily discernable.

Generally when designing the 8P 4-6-2 the normal parameters of BR Standard design were followed and they included ensuring the upmost in steam producing capacity permitted by weight and clearance restrictions, simplicity, visibility and accessibility, the number of moving parts reduced to a minimum and the simplification of shed maintenance by increased use of mechanical lubricators and grease lubrication and importantly a reduction in disposal time at sheds by the fitting of self cleaning smoke boxes, rocking grates and self-emptying ash pans.

The Harrow & Wealdstone Connection

That the new 8P 4-6-2 was ever built at all is an interesting railway story in its own right as it was a direct result of the fatal Harrow & Wealdstone crash, which happened on 8th October 1952. That horrific crash, which claimed 112 lives and injured approximately 350 persons, involved three steam hauled trains. The 07.31 local passenger train from Tring to Euston was standing in the up fast platform when it was hit in the rear by the fast approaching (approx 50-60 mph) 20.15 express sleeper train from Perth to Euston, the resulting carnage was horrendous. Seconds later however the double headed 08.00 down Euston-Liverpool express entered the station precincts at a speed of approximately 50mph. The down train footplate crew were unable to avoid a second catastrophic collision and to make matters much worse their train ploughed into the wreckage of the first two trains!

The locomotives hauling the Liverpool train were both damaged beyond repair; they were LMS Stanier Jubilee 4-6-0 No 45637 WINDWARD ISLANDS and LMS Stanier Princess Royal 4-6-2 No 46202 PRINCESS ANNE. Loco No 46202 had only some weeks earlier returned to service as a conventional locomotive having been rebuilt as a Princess Royal '8P' Pacific from the experimental steam turbine referred to as the 'Turbomotive'.

Riddles seized the opportunity

The seriously damaged Princess Royal class loco was declared to be beyond economic repair and that decision left a serious gap in the number of 8P locomotives available to BR. The situation thus provided the BR Standard Locomotive Group team leader, Mr R. A. Riddles, with the opportunity to introduce the prototype of his 8P Pacific Standard design. To facilitate the project special financial authorisation was given by the BR board. Riddles and his team anticipated that the new prototype 8P would become the forerunner of a larger class of such engines. In the event only one member of that class was built, No 71000 DUKE OF GLOUCESTER entered revenue earning service with BR (ex Crewe Works) in May 1954. Interestingly the loco designer's retirement from BR took place shortly before his 8P prototype emerged from the works.

Duke in BR Service

Over the years there has been a great deal written about the below expectation performances of this unique locomotive. With an early end to steam traction looming British Railways were reluctant at that time to address those problems, and in truth no great effort was made to rectify them.

However on the Swindon Test Plant No 71000 reportedly produced higher cylinder efficiency than any other simple expansion engine had recorded. That being 86% of what was in theory possible, when compared on the Rankine steam cycle, with a corresponding steam consumption figure of 12.2lb per indicated horsepower hour. During a test run carried out on the West of England mainline

Just arrived in Crewe station with 'The Mid-Day Scot' on 1 June 1956 (that day a late running arrival, through no fault of the loco) No 71000 attracts a lot of interest from enthusiasts young and old. The loco was replaced by Duchess Pacific 46236 CITY OF BRADFORD for the journey north of the border. 'The Mid-Day Scot' service ran between London Euston and Glasgow Central from 26 September 1927 to 9 September 1939 and again from 26 September 1949 until 13 June 1965. The use of a headboard on this Anglo Scottish service was introduced in the summer of 1951. Note the original style single footsteps above the buffer beam. *71000 Trust with the permission of photographer Peter Kerslake*

Standard 8P Pacific No 71000 DUKE OF GLOUCESTER is seen in a clean condition whilst being service between runs at Camden shed. Note the modified footstep above the buffer beam. (1B) in June 1962. *J.G. Dewing/Colour Rail*

between Swindon and Westbury 'The Duke' generally delighted observers with impressive performances both in the test plant, and on the road.

During the aforementioned trial run (and on analysing the recorded data) it became apparent that there was a fault somewhere in the 8P Pacific's design. Simply put when the loco reached a given rate of steam production (30,000 to 32,000 lb of steam per hour approximately depending of the quality of the coal used) the engine's firebox would just not burn appreciably more coal, no matter how hard the fireman worked to keep the box 'full up'. A solution to that problem was never found by British Railways and the 'Duke' went on to earn the tag 'poor steamer' during its 8½ years in revenue earning service.

The locomotive was to say the least not overly popular with footplate crews! The Crewe shed rumour mill had it that some drivers were said to have changed turns or even phoned in sick when faced with the prospect of being rostered to a 'heavy

Standard 8P Pacific No 71000 DUKE OF GLOUCESTER is pictured at Swindon on 31 October 1954 in the company of BR '9F' No 92001. The Riddles 8P Pacific visited Swindon Works during October 1954 and was run on the Swindon Test Plant in order to test the power output of the loco (steam producing capability etc). Thereafter the loco made an impressive test run out and back to Swindon which was a great example of fast running with a heavy train (20 coaches) however the test engineers described the loco's coal consumption as 'astronomical'.
K.C.H. Fairey/Colour Rail

Standard 8P Pacific No 71000 DUKE OF GLOUCESTER on an up WCML service near Winsford in June 1961. *Colin Whitfield/Rail Photoprints Collection*

train' turn of duty with the shy steaming No 71000. However, and supposedly against all the odds, when in the hands of skilful footplate crews No 71000 did turn in some very good performances. The 'Duke' regularly worked West Coast main line express services; in particular during the period 1956/8 the loco was often rostered to work the Crewe-Euston-Crewe section of prestigious Mid-Day Scot service.

'The Duke' was based at Crewe North shed (5A) for all of its operating life and was in its later years regularly employed on boat train and other express services on the undemanding North Wales Coast line between Crewe and Holyhead. In fact the last BR passenger turn for No 71000 was reportedly the 9.20am Crewe/Holyhead/Crewe stopping train. The locomotives reputation as a poor steamer followed it into what, with hindsight, many consider to have been premature retirement in November 1962.

Withdrawn, and almost cut up!
The steaming problems would be solved and the designer's faith in his 8P Pacific design justified, but not until many years later and then only after a great deal of hard work by the Duke of Gloucester's magnificent restoration team.

Standard 8P Pacific No 71000 DUKE OF GLOUCESTER is seen in a filthy condition 'on shed' at Holyhead (6J) in the summer of 1961. *Colour Rail*

When the locomotive was withdrawn it was initially selected to become one of the locomotives within the National Collection; however that plan was shelved for reasons best known to the museum authorities. However it was decided that the cylinders and valve gear were the only items worthy of saving and accordingly the left hand unit was removed and after being sectioned was placed on display at the Science Museum, Kensington. In order to restore balance during a move to the scrap yard the other cylinder was also removed.

The loco was purchased by Woodham Brothers of Barry South Wales for scrapping. Famously, due to an administrative error, the unwanted loco was at first sent to the wrong scrapyard. No 71000 was sent in error to Cashmores of Newport who had already started stripping the loco prior to cutting, but eagle eyed former BR fireman Maurice Shepherd on a visit to the yard noticed that the destination label on the condemned loco read 'Woodhams Barry'.

He then successfully persuaded the scrapmen to cease work on the 8P Pacific and check the documentation. This they did and as a consequence the condemned loco was later moved to what was intended to be its last resting place. The actions of Maurice Shepherd set in motion a move which almost certainly saved the engine as other 'work in progress' stopped Woodhams cutting the 'Duke' on its arrival at Barry, the loco then stood in their locomotive graveyard for approximately 7 years.

The hulk of 71000 pictured in Woodham Brothers Scrap yard Barry in November 1971. This image was taken to show that the outside cylinders had been removed. Back then the locos return to steam really could be called the 'Impossible Dream'. *Keith Langston*

An interesting picture of No 71000 taken when the loco was stored in Crewe North shed (5A) after being withdrawn and prior to its future being determined. You would be right to suspect that the loco is resting in a Southern Region shed because of the SR route indicator discs. That is however not the case, the discs are simply a spurious addition. Are you the railway man/enthusiast who placed them on the condemned loco back in 1962/3?
Colin Whitfield/Rail Photoprints Collection

The Impossible Dream

Corrosion and the attention of souvenir hunters took their toll on the condition of the hulk and by the time that the 71000 Preservation Society (formed 1974) made a successful bid to remove the 8P BR Standard from Barry there existed little more than the boiler, main frames, centre cylinder (minus cambox) and cab framework, even the withdrawn engines BR 1J tender had been removed and taken away to a steel works where its chassis was used for transporting steel products.

There were many at the time of the rescue who considered that the return to working order of No 71000 would turn out to be an impossible task. Apart from the obvious firebox and boiler refurbishments replacing the missing outside cylinders and associated Caprotti gear would, they reasoned, prove too costly and mean that the Duke of Gloucester would become a restoration 'bridge too far'. After all, said many the 'Duke' had proved to be a failure in traffic so how could restorationists overcome those problems? They of course got their answer when 13 years later the 'Duke' became a living breathing locomotive again.

The cost of the 'Duke' hulk, and a suitable tender was £4950 an amount raised by the ambitious restorationists and paid over to the scrapmen so that what

Standard 8P Pacific No 71000 DUKE OF GLOUCESTER is pictured southbound at Forton on the WCML in August 2005. This pan shot shows the distinctive lines of the BR Standard Class 8 to good effect. *Fred Kerr*

remained of the loco could leave Barry, which it did on 24th April 1974. When first rescued the locomotive was taken to the Great Central Railway at Loughborough.

During the restoration process the 'poor steamer' claims which had bedeviled the loco during its short and unspectacular working life were investigated and the rectification of any faults found were placed high on the 'Trusts' list of priorities. The engineers made what they believed to be two significant discoveries, both of which British Railways had either not been aware of and/or because of the anticipated only short service life predicted for the 8P chose not to address.

Firstly the restorers deduced that the chimney on the 'Duke' was too small when compared to those fitted to other locomotives of a similar size resulting in poor boiler draughting during times of high steam demand. Secondly they discovered that the firebed (grate) air inlet dampers had not been manufactured correctly and were not as specified on the original BR Derby design, they were in fact too small and that crucial mistake led to poor air supply to the fire resulting in inefficient combustion. Obviously the combination of both faults went some way to explaining the poor steaming claims. However those few words describe only briefly what a mammoth undertaking the restoration of No 71000 was and images of the loco before removal from Barry offer a stark reminder of the daunting and challenging task faced by the 71000 Preservation Society.

Having corrected the two major BR manufacturing errors the restorationists also included in their rebuild a type of Kylchap exhaust system which had first been suggested to BR in the 1955 but not acted upon. Of course there were also many potential performance enhancing modifications carried out including a later enlargement of the blast pipes diameter, all of which collectively meant that the rebuilt 'Duke' which returned to the mainline was a far superior locomotive than the one originally outshopped from Crewe Works. Reportedly some footplate men who had experience of the loco in both its 'lives' were open in their praise of the rebuild describing it as being unrecognisable from the poor steamer which operated out of Crewe North between 1954 and 1962.

The complicated and groundbreaking restoration of No 71000 is well documented elsewhere and was in the main only made possible by the generosity of thousands of enthusiasts and well wishers. Initially the Science Museum contributed £6000 towards the cost of the cylinders and valve gear and during the later days of the project Crewe Borough Council also made donations to the restoration fund. Trust members and others held a multiplicity of fund raising events and further finance was also raised by a share issue.

In 1977 the 71000 Preservation Society was superseded by a pair of newly constituted bodies namely 71000 Steam Locomotive Ltd which was a company in which people wishing to further support the project could buy shares and The 71000 (Duke of Gloucester) Steam Locomotive Trust which was set up as a registered charity. The locomotive was placed in trust to the later organisation.

Standard 8P Pacific No 71000 DUKE OF GLOUCESTER is pictured heading for Carlisle along the picturesque Cumbrian Coast Route in July 2010 with a HF Railtours charter. Note the wisp of steam to the rear of the tender indicating that the fireman is employing the steam operated coal pusher. *Fred Kerr*

The 'Duke' is pictured with its support coach running south under the wires through Acton Bridge station on the WCML. Note The Mid-Day Scot, Crewe Phoenix, 5A Crewe North shed plate and SC self cleaning smoke box indicator below the shed plate. *Keith Langston*

The 'Duke' hurries through Winsford heading south on the 25 November 1995 with the 'BBC Radio Merseyside Children in Need' special. The swirling exhaust almost hides the Class 47 No 47768 Resonant coupled inside the BR 8P Pacific. *Sue Langston*

Locomotive designer Mr. R.A. Riddles visited Loughborough in 1981 to check on the progress of the rebuild of 'his' 8P Pacific. During the visit he told the team that they had 'better get it finished soon or you'll have to start restoring me!' Unfortunately he was right, Mr. Riddles did not live to see his unique design steam in traffic again as he passed away some three years before that memorable occasion. The completed locomotive was officially recommissioned by 'His Royal Highness the Duke of Gloucester' during a memorable event held at Rothley station, GCR on 11th November 1986. The impossible dream had that day been realised.

Standard 8P Pacific No 71000 DUKE OF GLOUCESTER leaving Workington on 24 February 2007, after a water stop whilst working the Railway Touring Company "Cumbrian Coast Pullman" charter from Manchester Victoria to Carlisle via Barrow and Cumbrian Coast. *Fred Kerr*

The BR 'book' manufacturing cost of the prototype Pacific was recorded as being £44,655. The cost of rebuilding 3-cylinder the engine was said to have been £105,000 with a further £65,000 having been estimated as the value of free work carried out and components supplied. However the true commercial cost of the many manufactured parts supplied would probably have been at least double that total.

On completion the 'Duke' returned to the mainline and some 25 years later (and after other rebuild work and ongoing maintenance) No 71000 is still thrilling enthusiasts nationwide with some spirited mainline runs, additionally the locomotive's regular appearances at preserved railways are greatly enjoyed.

The restored locomotive has graced national network metals all over the country and when doing so has carried many historically important headboards, and a selection of new ones the impressive list includes (in addition to the famous Crewe Phoenix) 'Cumbrian Mountain Express', 'The Mid-Day Scot', 'The Red Dragon', 'The North Wales Coast Express', 'The Midlander', 'The Moorlander', 'Cumbrian Mountain Express', 'The Thames Clyde Express', 'The Royal Shakespeare', 'The South Yorkshireman', 'The Carillion' and 'The Red Rose' mentions of which will no doubt bring back fond memories to both old and young railway enthusiasts.

United again, loco restorationist Keith Collier spent all of his adult life at Crewe Works and regularly carried out work on the Standards built there, which of course included No 71000. Keith went on to become an active member of the magnificent Duke restoration team, thereafter served for a time on the loco's mainline support crew and in 2012 is still actively involved with steam traction mainline operations. He is pictured in the loco's driving seat as 71000 visited the 'Works' for the 2004 Great Gathering event. *Keith Langston*

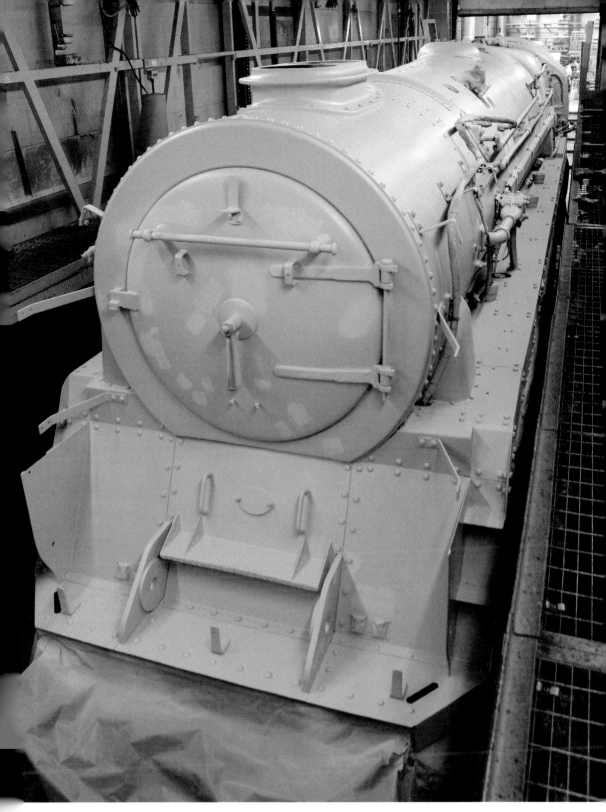

In July 2004 'The Duke' returned to Crewe Works (then a division of Bombardier Transportation) in order to be painted with a new high class livery. The loco is pictured in the paint shop having been spray coated with a primer. *Keith Langston*

Duke of Gloucester class facts

8P 71000 4-6-2 BR Standard 'Duke of Gloucester'

Introduced: 1954

Designer: Riddles designed at Derby

Company: British Railways-Built Crewe

Weight: 101 ton 5 cwt

Tender: Original weight 55 ton 10 cwt, later Modified to 53 ton 14 cwt

Driving Wheel: 6 foot 2 inches diameter

Boiler Pressure: 250psi superheated

Cylinders: Three 18 inch diameter x 28 inch stroke

Tractive Effort: 39080lbf

Valve Gear: Caprotti

Caprotti Valve Gear

Caprotti valve gear is a distinctively different type of steam locomotive valve gear which was invented and first introduced by Italian engineer Arturo Caprotti. The system uses camshaft and associated poppet valves rather than the various types of piston valves more conventionally used by locomotive designers/builders. The Caprotti system was based on valves used in internal combustion engine design which Caprotti significantly changed to make the method suitable for the use with steam engines.

In the 1950s the system was further improved and the resulting equipment from that development became known as British Caprotti valve gear. Caprotti valve gear was fitted to the last two British Railways built Black Fives No's 44686/7, the last 30 BR Standard Class 5s, numbers 73125-54 and Riddles prototype 3-cylinder Class 8P Pacific 71000 Duke of Gloucester.

Caprotti valve gear is said to facilitate a more efficient use of generated steam and benefits of the Caprotti system include the fact that much of the mechanism is enclosed, a factor which practically speaking means a reduction in damage cause by wear and tear in the harsh steam locomotive environment. The use of Caprotti poppet valve gear also allows independent control of the locomotive cylinders admission and exhaust functions. An important downside to the system is the cost of manufacture which is often stated as being considerably higher than that for conventional piston valves gear.

Perhaps the most striking difference to the lineside observer was the addition of British Caprotti rotary cam poppet valve gear to the cylinders, driven by shafts attached to the centre driving wheels and connected to cam boxes. In this comparison shot the Duke's Caprotti gear can be compared with the conventionally valve gear of Jubilee No 5690 Leander. *Keith Langston*

Standard 8P Pacific No 71000 DUKE OF GLOUCESTER pictured at Acton Bridge (WCML) with a southbound 'Dalesman' charter train. That working would bring the 8P to Crewe and therefore in position to attend the September 2005 Great Gathering as one of the 'Made in Crewe' star attractions. *Keith Langston*

'The Duke' is seen on Crewe Works prior to the 2004 Great Gathering event and is in the company of another Crewe built loco Stanier Mogul NO 42968. Long serving 71000 Group engineer Gary Shannon is preparing the loco for an examination of the inside cylinder. *Keith Langston*

Standard 8P Pacific No 71000 DUKE OF GLOUCESTER is pictured when newly arrived at Crewe Works for the '2004 GG' event and after hauling The Dalesman charter. The 'Duke' is in the company of Crewe built Jubilee 4-6-0 No 5690 (45690) LEANDER. *Keith Langston*

On the 'Works' the 'Duke' is shunted onto the coaling point at the September 2004 Great Gathering by Llangollen Railway based 0-6-0 Saddle Tank JESSIE. *Keith Langston*

Chapter 3

6P5F 4-6-2
BR STANDARD 'CLAN'

BR Standard Clan class 4-6-2 No 72005 CLAN MACGREGOR is pictured in action well away from 'her' normal stamping grounds. The loco is passing under the former 'Birdcage' at Rugby with an up parcels train, a 'Clan' that far south was a rare occurrence, October 1954. *J. M. Chamney/Colour Rail*

This picture of No 72005 taken in the shed yard at Glasgow Corkerhill (67A) shows clearly the higher running plate, smaller diameter boiler, taller steam dome and chimney, also the folded concertina 'draught screen' fitted between the engine cab and tender can be seen. *David Anderson*

The Clans

Between 1951 and 1952 ten lighter versions of the Britannia class were constructed, they were the Standard 'Class 6' 6MT 4-6-2 Clans and accordingly were named after 10 Scottish Clans. The new class had higher running plates, smaller diameter boilers and taller steam domes and chimneys than their '7MT' cousins. However the Crewe built 'small' Pacific's were not as successful as their bigger cousins and in fact were generally considered to be poor machines lacking anything like the punch of the Britannia's.

The thinking behind the Standard 'Class 6' design centred on the need to provide a Pacific type locomotive for use on the routes which prohibited the use of the larger Class 7 4-6-2 engines, because of axle loading restrictions. The smaller Clan boiler was carried on the same chassis as the Britannia class engines and the achieved lower axle loading was as a consequence only 19 tons in full working order, i.e. 1½ tons per axle lighter than the Class 7's. The tenders used were the same as those supplied to the first batch of Britannias, designated BR1 they had a water capacity of 4250 gallons and a 7 ton capacity coal space. As with the Standard Class 7 Pacific's draught screens were later fitted between the engine cab and tender.

All of the Crewe built class were allocated to the Scottish Region but did not, as anticipated, work regularly over the testing Highland Line due to a lack of adhesive power, but instead worked mainly on Glasgow-Manchester/Liverpool express services. Examples of the class were briefly trialed on the Midland Main Line and also on the Great Eastern routes to Ipswich and Norwich.

The 6P5F's below par performances in traffic coupled with the quickening pace of dieselisation caused a planned order for a further fifteen of the class to be cancelled and those locomotives, if built, would have been numbers 72010 - 72014 allocated to BR Southern Region and 72015–72024 for the BR Scottish Region.

Locomotives numbered 72000–72004 were taken out of service in 1962, numbers72005, 72007 and 72009 in 1965 whilst 72006 and 72008 lasted until 1966. None were preserved but however a long standing project to build a new 'Clan' 4-6-2 was reportedly still in its initial stages during 2012. See www.72010-hengist.org

BR Standard Clan class 4-6-2 No 72004 CLAN MACDONALD is pictured 'out of region' and on shed at Bank Hall (27A) on 14 July 1957. Bank Hall shed was in Bootle, Liverpool and presumably the Standard 6P5F was serviced there after working to Merseyside with an express ex Glasgow. Note the BR Scottish Region light blue backed smoke box number plate and shed plate. *M.J. Reade/Colour Rail*

Clan Class Facts

BR Pacific 'Clan' Class 6P5F (7MT) 4-6-2

Built: Crewe Works 1951–52, 10 locomotives built.

Loco Weight: 86 tons 19 cwt

Tenders: BR1 49 tons 3 cwt

Driving Wheels Diameter: 6 foot 2 inches

Boiler Pressure: 225lb/psi

Cylinders: (2) 19½ inch diameter x 28 inch stroke

Valve Gear (Piston Valves): Walschaerts

Coal Capacity: BR1 7 tons

Water Capacity: BR1 4250 gallons

Tractive Effort: 27520lb at (85% pressure)

Scottish Clans

In naming the first ten BR Standard Clan class locomotives the decision makers had a great many names to choose from and it is unclear what criteria were applied in order to choose the ten which were decided upon. There are Highland and Lowland clans and collectively they are split into two distinct groups basically being those with, and those without chiefs. A clan must firstly be recognized by the *Court of the Lord Lyon* and thereafter if it does not have a chief recognized by the *Lord Lyon King of Arms* it is referred to as being an Armigerous Clan. *The Court of the Lord Lyon*, also known as the *Lyon Court*, is a standing court of law which regulates heraldry in Scotland. Note, *Armigerous* from *arminger,* noun, esquire and person entitled to bear heraldic arms.

The numerous Scottish Clans owe their origins to Celtic, Norse or Norman-French traditions and by the 13th century clans were firmly established in the various regions of Scotland. The broad meaning of the word 'Clan', with Gaelic origins, is family and/or children although it should be understood that not everyone in the same clan were necessarily related to each other. Many clans can be traced back to a specific part of Scotland.

The clans mainly lived off the land with cattle and livestock ownership being their main source of wealth. It was not uncommon for inter clan unrest to occur, often prompted by disputes concerning the ownership of free ranging cattle and the violation of jealously guarded historically important borders. History shows that the most important clan chiefs exercised real power over the lands which they controlled. Chiefs have been described variously as being part king, part protectorate and very certainly the ultimate judge and jury.

BR Standard Clan class 4-6-2 No 72007 CLAN MACKINTOSH is seen at Lancaster Green Ayre with an RCTS 'Riddle-Lune' railtour on Saturday 23 May 1964. *Len Mills*

The clan system survived almost unchanged until the time of the very bloody Battle of Culloden (1746) where the Jacobite rebellion was crushed by troops loyal to King George II. Trade and improved communications between the northern clans and the 'Sassenachs' (those of Saxon origin) in the south began, over time, to erode the insularity of the clan system. Many historians consider that the effective end of the clan system came about as a result of the infamous 'Highland Clearances', when thousands of Scottish agricultural workers were forced out of their crofts (farms) and sought the promise of a better life away from their native land.

The Locomotives

72000 CLAN BUCHANAN built Crewe Works, entered service December 1951 with a BR1 4250 gallon tender, withdrawn from BR service in December 1962. Cut for scrap by BR Darlington Works in March 1964.

Clan Buchanan is an Armigerous Scottish clan whose origins are said to lie in the 1225 grant of lands on the eastern shore of Loch Lomond to clergyman Sir Absalon of Buchanan by the Earl of Lennox. Clan motto, *Clarior Hinc Honos* – Brighter Hence the Honour.

BR Standard Clan class 4-6-2 No 72000 CLAN BUCHANAN pictured when in full cry on the West Coast Main Line (WCML) between Crawford and Elvanfoot, with a Glasgow Central to Blackpool holiday relief on 11 April 1960. *David Anderson*

72001 CLAN CAMERON built Crewe Works, entered service December 1951 with a BR1 4250 gallon tender, withdrawn from BR service in December 1962. Cut for scrap by BR Darlington Works in February 1964.

Clan Cameron is a West Highland Scottish clan, with one main branch Lochiel, and numerous cadet branches. The Clan Cameron traditional lands are in Lochaber and encompass the mountain Ben Nevis, the highest mountain in the British Isles. The chief of the clan is customarily referred to as simply 'Lochiel'. Clan motto, *Aonaibh Ri Cheile* – Unite.

In this autumn 1958 picture BR Standard Clan class 4-6-2 No 72001 CLAN CAMERON is seen on Glasgow Central – Manchester/Liverpool express duty passing between Crawford and Elvanfoot on the WCML. *David Anderson*

72002 CLAN CAMPBELL built Crewe Works, entered service January 1952 with a BR1 4250 gallon tender, withdrawn from BR service in December 1962. Cut for scrap by BR Darlington Works in April 1964.

Clan Campbell is a Highland Scottish clan. Historically one of the largest, most powerful and most successful of all the Highland clans, the Campbell lands were in Argyll and the chief of the clan became the Earl and later Duke of Argyll. Clan motto, *Ne Obliviscaris* – Forget Not.

BR Standard Clan class 4-6-2 No 72002 CLAN CAMPBELL is seen on shed at Perth (63A) on 2 June 1956 having worked in from Glasgow Buchanan Street with a parcels train. *David Anderson*

72003 CLAN FRASER built Crewe Works, entered service January 1952 with a BR1 4250 gallon tender, withdrawn from BR service in December 1962. Cut for scrap by BR Darlington Works in March 1964.

Clan Fraser is a Scottish clan of French origin. The Clan has been strongly associated with Inverness and the surrounding area since the Clan's founder gained lands there in the 13th century. Since its founding, the Clan has been prominent in local politics and was active in every major military conflict involving Scotland. 'Fraser' is reportedly the most prominent family name within the Inverness area. Clan motto Je Suis Prest – I Am Ready.

BR Standard Clan class 4-6-2 No 72003 CLAN FRASER works hard on the climb to Beattock Summit, with a Liverpool/Manchester – Glasgow Central express on 18 April 1959. *David Anderson*

72004 CLAN MACDONALD built Crewe Works, entered service February 1952 with a BR1 4250 gallon tender, withdrawn from BR service in December 1962. Cut for scrap at BR Darlington Works March 1964.

Clan Macdonald is one of the largest Scottish clans with numerous branches. Several of which have chiefs recognized by the *Lord Lyon King of Arms*; they are Clan Macdonald of Sleat, Clan Macdonald of Clanranald, Clan MacDonell of Glengarry, Clan MacDonald of Keppoch, and Clan MacAlister. Notable branches without chiefs (Armigerous Clan) are the MacDonalds of Dunnyveg, MacDonalds of Lochalsh, the MacDonalds of Glencoe, and the MacDonalds of Ardnamurchan. The MacDonnells of Antrim do not belong to the Scottish associations and they have a chief officially recognized in Ireland. Clan motto, *Per Mare Per Terra* – By Sea and By Land

BR Standard Clan class 4-6-2 No 72004 CLAN MACDONALD looks to be making heavy weather of the 4 coach Carlisle – Glasgow Central stopping train when pictured on the WCML north of Harthope, Beattock Bank on 18 April 1959. *David Anderson*

72005 CLAN MACGREGOR built Crewe Works, entered service February 1952 with a BR1 4250 gallon tender, withdrawn from BR service in May 1965. Cut for scrap by Arnott Young of Troon in July 1965.

Clan MacGregor (Clan Gregor, Clan McGregor, Clan M'Gregor is a Highland clan. It is the most senior clan of Siol Alpin (Seed of Alpin) referring to King Kenneth I, descending from the ancient Kings of the Picts and Dál Riata. This clan was famously outlawed for nearly 200 years after a power struggle with the Clan Campbell. Clan motto, *S Rioghal Mo Dhream* - Royal is my Race.

BR Standard Clan class 4-6-2 No 72005 CLAM MACGREGOR passes under the wonderful signal gantry at Carstairs with a London–Perth train in August 1958. Note the new 'Horsebox' immediately behind the smartly turned out loco. *David Anderson*

72006 CLAN MACKENZIE built Crewe Works, entered service February 1952 with a BR1 4250 gallon tender, withdrawn from BR service in May 1966. Cut for scrap by McWilliams of Shettleston in October 1966.

Clan Mackenzie is a Highland Scottish clan, traditionally associated with Kintail and adjacent lands in Ross-shire. It was a powerful clan of Celtic stock and was not amongst the clans that originated from Norman ancestry. The clan was recorded as residing in a stronghold at Eilean Donan on Loch Duich. There were also clan strongholds at Kilcoy Castle and Brahan Castle and the Mackenzies of Tarbat had their seat at Castle Leod, in Strathpeffer in the 17th century. Clan motto, *Luceo Non Uro* – I Shine Not Burn.

BR Standard Clan class 4-6-2 No 72006 CLAN MACKENZIE pictured on shed at Stranraer (67F) on 18 August 1962. *K.C.H. Fairey/Colour Rail*

72007 CLAN MACKINTOSH built Crewe Works, entered service March 1952 with a BR1 4250 gallon tender, withdrawn from BR service in December 1965. Cut for scrap by Campbells of Airdrie in March 1966.

Clan Mackintosh is a Scottish clan from Inverness traditionally with strong Jacobite ties. The Mackintoshes were also chiefs of the Chattan Confederation. Seathach, son of Donnchadh Mac Duibh, accompanied King Malcolm IV of Scotland to Morayshire to suppress rebellion in 1160. In 1163 he was granted land in the Findhorn valley and made constable of Inverness Castle. Upon Seathach's death in 1179, his son Shaw, the second, became chief. Clan Motto, *Touch Not the Cat Bot a Glove* – Touch Not the Cat Without a Glove.

BR Standard Clan class 4-6-2 No 72007 CLAN MACKINTOSH has a Liverpool/Manchester–Glasgow Central express at Auchencastle on Beattock Bank, 7 July 1958. Note that the second coach is a 12 wheel restaurant car. *David Anderson*

72008 CLAN MACLEOD built Crewe Works, entered service March 1952 with a BR1 4250 gallon tender, withdrawn from BR service in April 1966. Cut for scrap by McWilliams of Shettleston in June 1966.

Clan Macleod is a Highland Scottish clan mainly associated with the Isle of Skye. There are two main branches of the clan: the Macleods of Harris and Dunvegan, whose chief is Macleod of Macleod, and the Macleods of Lewis, whose chief is Macleod of The Lewes. Both branches claim descent from Leòd, who lived in the 13th century. Clan motto, *Hold Fast* – Stand Your Ground.

BR Standard Clan class 4-6-2 No 72008 CLAN MACLEOD had only weeks to remain in service when pictured in a very rough exterior condition at Perth shed (63A) on 18 September 1965, the nameplates have been removed. *David Anderson*

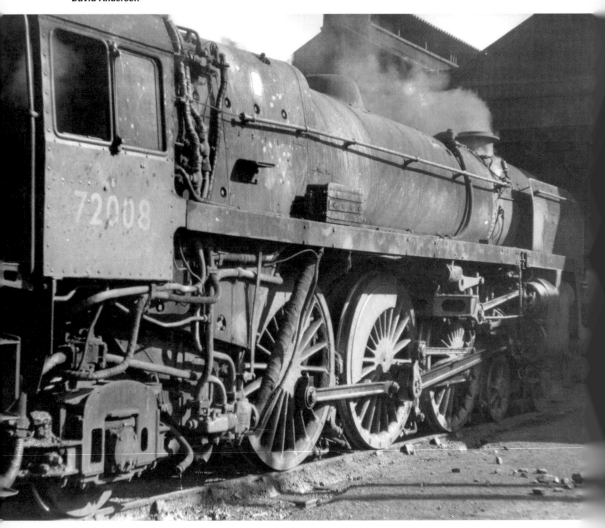

72009 CLAN STEWART built Crewe Works, entered service April 1952 with a BR1 4250 gallon tender, withdrawn from BR service in August 1965. Cut for scrap by Motherwell Machinery & Scrap, Wishaw in December 1965.

Clan Stewart is a Highland clan. The clan is recognized by the Court of the Lord Lyon, however it does not have a clan chief recognized by the Lord Lyon King of Arms. Because the clan has no chief it can be considered an armigerous clan; however the Earls of Galloway are in modern times considered to be the principal branch of this clan. The Court of the Lord Lyon recognizes two other Stewart clans, Clan Stuart of Bute and Clan Stewart of Appin. Clan motto, *Furth Fortune and Fill the Fetters.*

BR Standard Clan class 4-6-2 No 72009 CLAN STEWART a Carlisle Kingmoor (then 68A) prepares to leave Carstairs Junction Station with the 9.30am Glasgow Central to Liverpool/Manchester express (10.17 am from Carstairs) on 9 April 1955. *David Anderson*

Chapter 4

BR STANDARD
5 MT 4-6-0 'CLASS 5'

The BR Standard Doncaster designed 'Class 5' 5MT 4-6-0 types were produced between 1951 and 1957 and the 172 locomotives given the number series 73000 to 73171. The design was based on the LMS type 'Black Fives' and the new class of engines was intended to initially augment and then eventually replace that class plus the LNER type B1's, the GWR type Halls and the SR type King Arthur Class. Consequently the Standard Class 5's were sent to all regions of British Railways.

Ready for inspection! Brand new and ex Derby works, BR Standard Class 5 No 73000 is pictured at Neasden (then 34E) prior to inspection by the railway top brass at Marylebone station. Note that the first of the class is coupled with a BR1 tender. *C.C.B. Herbert/Colour Rail*

In the first instance Riddles and his Standard Design Group considered producing a 'Class 5' 2-cylinder (19 ½ inch x 28 inch) Pacific (4-6-2) with a working boiler pressure of 225psi (superheated). In order to have the widest possible route availability the proposed 4-6-2 would only have had an 18 ton axle load. The designer's first thoughts were to construct the loco with a wide grate, utilise bar frames and incorporate a double chimney and blast pipe. The proposal begs the question, given that the Class 6P5F Clans were referred to as 'Small Pacifics' would the 'Class 5' 4-6-2s have been referred to a 'Mini Pacifics'?

As the preliminary design work got underway the new specification was changed to one for a 4-6-0 locomotive. However the design did incorporate certain parts in common with the Clans and also included a version of the Ivatt improved Stanier LMS Black Five boiler design, which in traffic had proved itself to be an excellent steam producer (designated BR3). The cylinders (2 outside 19 inch x 28 inch) valve gear and coupled wheels were essentially the same as the Class 6P5F Pacific's and conventional Walschaert valve gear was chosen for the majority of the class, however a later batch (locos 73125–73154) were fitted with similar Caprotti valve gear to the prototype BR Standard 8P Pacific No 71000.

In line with all the Standard types they were successful engines, many incorporating cut away tender sides to improve vision when running tender first. The Standards were easier to maintain and service, being fitted with standard self cleaning features.

Twenty of the BR Southern Region 73000 allocated engines received names whilst in British Railways service.

A later batch of Standard Class 5 4-6-0 locos (73125 – 73154) were fitted with similar Caprotti valve gear to the prototype BR Standard 8P Pacific No 71000. Loco No 73135 is seen on shed at Stockport Edgeley (9B) in June 1965, this 1956 built loco continued in BR service until April 1968. Note that the engine is coupled to a BR1C tender. *Keith Langston*

Standard Class 5 4-6-0 build details

Loco Numbers	Build location	Year
73000–73004	Derby Works	1951
73005–73009	Derby Works	1951
73010–73029	Derby Works	1951/52
73030–73039	Derby Works	1952/53
73040–73049	Derby Works	1953
73050–73074	Derby Works	1954
73075–73099	Derby Works	1955
73100–73109	Doncaster Works	1955/56
73110–73119	Doncaster Works	1955
73120–73124	Doncaster Works	1956
73125–73144	Derby Works	1956
73145–73154*	Derby Works	1957
73155–73159	Doncaster Works	1956/57
73160–73171	Doncaster Works	1957

*73154 was the last steam locomotive to be built at Derby Works.

BR Standard 5 MT 4-6-0 'Class 5' class facts

4-6-0 BR Standard 'Class 5' - 172 locomotives built

Introduced: 1951–1957

Designer: Riddles. Parent office for the design Doncaster

Company: British Railways

Weight: 76 ton 4 cwt

Tender: BR1 49 ton 3 cwt, BR1B 50 ton 5 cwt, BR1C 53 ton 5 cwt, BR1F 55 ton 5 cwt, BR1G 52 ton 10 cwt, BR1H 49 ton 3 cwt

Driving Wheel: 6 foot 2 inches diameter

Boiler Pressure: 225psi superheated

Cylinders: 19 inch diameter x 28 inch stroke

Tractive Effort: 26120lbf

Valve Gear: Walschaert piston valves – 30 locos Caprotti poppet valves

BR Standard Class 5 No 73012 was a Swindon allocated (82C) engine when pictured heading a Swindon – Birmingham car parts train at Oxford in May 1961. *David Anderson*

Original tender type allocations

Loco numbers	Tender type	Coal	Water Capacity
73000–73049	BR1 inset	7 ton	4250 gallon
73050–73052	BR1G inset	7 ton	5000 gallon
73053–73064	BR1H inset	7 ton	4250 gallon
73065–73079	BR1C curved top flush sided	9 ton	4725 gallon
73080–73089	BR1B curved top flush sided	7 ton	4725 gallon
73090–73099	BR1C curved top flush sided	9 ton	4725 gallon
73100–73109	BR1B curved top flush sided	7 ton	4725 gallon
73110–73119	BR1F curved top high sided	7 ton	5625 gallon
73120–73134	BR1B curved top flush sided	7 ton	4725 gallon
73135–73144	BR1C curved top flush sided	9 ton	4725 gallon
73145–73171	BR1B curved top flush sided	7 ton	4725 gallon

Tenders as coupled to BR Standard locomotive types varied and in the main were interchangeable within a particular class and in some instances even between engine types. Some of the variations were not always visibly obvious, for example the BR2 and BR2A tenders as fitted to the Class 4MT 4-6-0 types were both 3500 gallon/6 ton capacity inset tenders however the BR2A version incorporated a hinged fall plate which when lowered located on top of the footplate floor, whilst the BR2 unit did not.

Liveries

The first locomotive No 73000 was given a black livery with LNWR style lining out, however only a single fine red line was applied to the side of the running plate, extending from cab to buffer beam. Interestingly the second loco in the number series, No 73001, received an altered version of the livery which included full lining out in red, grey and cream, along the running plate angle from buffer beam to cab. Some of the Southern Region allocated locomotives were, after general repairs, outshopped from Eastleigh Works with a fully lined green livery, but that was more the exception than the rule.

Locomotives equipped with French TIA water softening apparatus were originally identified by the way of a yellow spot painted just below the cab side number. However the spot was later changed to a triangle, in order to avoid confusion with the relevant Western Region (ex GWR) route availability code.

Modifications

The Southern Region allocated locomotive's tenders were treated as a special case in that there were no water troughs on that region and therefore higher water capacity tenders were a distinct advantage. Additionally extra lamp brackets were provided in positions typical of other Southern Region engines, i.e. fitted on either side of the locomotive smokebox door and on the rear of the tender. To facilitate other regional variations Standard Class 5 locos allocated to Weymouth (82F) were fitted with dual lamp brackets (ex Great Western Railway and ex Southern Railway style) in all positions. Some of the BR Southern Region allocated locomotives were also fitted with raised sand box covers (above the running plate).

As originally built the BR Class 5 locos had their driving wheels mounted on hollow axles and were fitted with forged 'I' section coupling rods. During later modifications newly supplied solid core axles were incorporated and in some

The BR Standard Class 5 engines were designed to replace the by then ageing Stanier Black Fives. Derby built loco No 73073 is pictured 'head to head' with Black Five No 45374, The Armstrong Whitworth1937 built Stanier loco was withdrawn from BR service in October 1967 (approx 30 years in traffic) interestingly No 73073 was withdrawn in that same month (approx 13 years in traffic). Note that the modified style of flat solid section coupling rods fitted to the BR Class 5 can clearly be seen in this July 1967 image taken on shed at Patricroft (then 9H). *Keith Langston*

instances the original style of coupling rods were retained whilst other locos, after axle changes, received new plain section coupling rods. The original choice of whistle for the class was a chime whistle which was located immediately behind the chimney. Later locomotives received normal BR 'bell type' whistles which were mounted on top of the firebox. As with the previous standard class builds these locos were over time fitted with concertina type draught excluders between cab and tender.

Two of the class Nos 73030/31 were delivered into service fitted with Westinghouse brakes for use on the same fitted freight trials on which Britannia locos No 70043/44 had previously been used (see that section). In the case of both the Class 5 locomotives only one compressor was fitted and located on the right hand side of the smokebox with a reservoir being located below the right hand running plate at the cab end. After undertaking the trials the Westinghouse brake gear was removed from the engines and they were returned to traffic as originally designed.

In traffic

The class were considered to be highly successful by locomotive crews and were equally popular with motive power depot personnel on all of the BR regions. The Standard Class 5s were considered to be more than capable of putting in exceptional performances when handled correctly. The class were declared to be worthy successors to the Stanier Black Fives they were designed to replace. In particular the Caprotti valve geared engines were especially highly thought of and were often described as being extremely strong, and very reliable in traffic.

Original locomotive regional allocations

London Midland Region

73000–73004, 73010–73029, 73040–73049, 73053–73054, 73065–73074, 73090–73099, 73135–73144

Scottish Region

73005–73009, 73030–73039, 73055–73064, 73075–73079, 73100–73109, 73120–73124, 73145–73154

Southern Region

73050–73052, 73080–73089, 73110–73119

Western Region

73125–73134

Eastern/North Eastern Regions

73155–73159, 73160–73171

Eastfield (65A) allocated BR Standard Class 5 No 73078 is pictured at the old Fort William station on 7 June 1957. That station was later demolished to make way for a new road system and railway station, work which was completed in 1975. *L.F. Folkard/Colour Rail*

BR Standard Class 5 No 73001 was still in original condition on 17 May 1961 when seen at Oxford with a Swindon–Birmingham car parts train. *David Anderson*

Named BR Standard Class 5 4-6-0 locomotives

Between 1918 and 1927 the London & South Western Railway (LSWR), under Urie and later the Southern Railway (SR) under Maunsell, introduced a class of 2-cylinder 5P 4-6-0 locomotives designated as 'N15' class.

Sir Herbert Walker, who was General Manager of the Southern Railway from 1923 until 1937 (and thereafter a director), had been mightily impressed by the LNERs new Pacifics and the GWRs Castles and thus charged his public relations team (under John Elliot) to come up with names for the 'N15' class which would 'capture the imagination of the regions rail travelling public'. Given that the 'Southern' had a route which passed close by Tintagel Castle in Cornwall, Elliot decided on a 'Court of Camelot' scheme for the names. Accordingly the N15 locos became commonly referred to as the 'King Arthur' class.

Following a British Railways Southern Region staff suggestion (in May 1958) which met with the approval of the regional management team, names from the withdrawn King Arthur 4-6-0 engines were selected to be recycled, and were then used on 20 of the newly introduced BR Standard Class 5 locos. The chosen N15 names were from locos numbers Nos 30736-55. The former SR 'N15' class locomotives whose names were chosen for recycling were withdrawn by BR between 1957 and 1958.

The names were allocated to the individual locomotives, six months plus later and without official ceremony, the nameplates were fitted as the chosen locomotives routinely passed through Eastleigh Works. The nameplates were similar to those on the original King Arthurs but did not carry the legend 'King Arthur Class'. The plates were to say the least 'unpretentious' and often extremely difficult to read from the lineside, especially on 'traffic dirty' locos.

Five examples of the class are preserved No 73050 home base Nene Valley Railway where the engine has been named CITY OF PETERBOROUGH, No 73082 BR name CAMELOT, home base Bluebell Railway, 73096 home base Mid Hants

Named BR Standard Class 5 4-6-0 No 73083 CAMELOT is pictured ''between turns' at Didcot in September 1964. The 'small' nameplate, with the former 'King Arthur' class name, can be seen on the running plate below the centre line of the steam dome. This locomotive is a preserved example. *David Anderson*

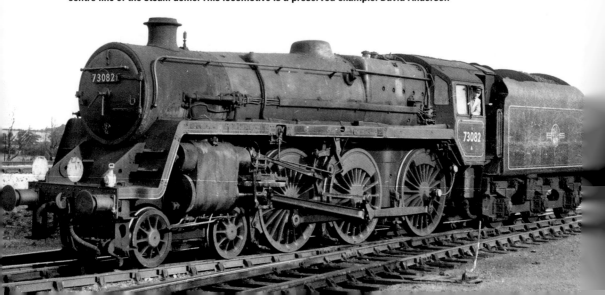

Named BR Standard 5 class locomotives

BR Number	Name	N15 number	BR Named	BR in traffic dates
73080	MERLIN	30740	02/1961	06/1955–07/1966
73081	EXCALIBUR	30736	02/1961	07/1955–07/1966
73082	CAMELOT	30742	08/1959	07/1955–06/1966
73083	PENDRAGON	30746	10/1959	07/1955–09/1966
73084	TINTAGEL	30745	10/1959	08/1955–12/1965
73085	MELISANDE	30753	08/1959	08/1955–07/1967
73086	THE GREEN KNIGHT	30754	12/1959	09/1955–10/1966
73087	LINETTE	30752	05/1961	09/1955–10/1966
73088	JOYOUS GARD	30741	05/1961	09/1955–10/1966
73089	MAID OF ASTOLAT	30744	05/1959	09/1955–09/1966
73110	THE RED KNIGHT	30755	01/1960	10/1955–01/1967
73111	KING UTHER	30737	02/1961	10/1955–09/1965
73112	MORGAN LE FAY	30750	04/1960	10/1955–06/1965
73113	LYONNESSE	30743	12/1959	10/1955–01/1967
73114	ETARRE	30751	03/1960	11/1955–06/1966
73115	KING PELLINORE	30738	01/1960	11/1955–03/1967
73116	ISEULT	30749	09/1962	11/1955–11/1964
73117	VIVIEN	30748	04/1961	11/1955–03/1967
73118	KING LEODEGRANCE	30739	02/1960	12/1955–07/1967
73119	ELAINE	30747	06/1959	12/1955–03/1967

Railway, No 73129 a Caprotti example, home base Midland Railway Centre and No 73156, home base the Great Central Railway. The first four of these locomotives have all steamed in preservation whilst No 73156 was under initial restoration in 2012. See also www.73156standard5group.co.uk

Disposal

The first of the class to be withdrawn was loco No 73027, a Derby built loco which entered service in December 1951, and was withdrawn in February 1964. The full complement of 172 engines were all in service from the end of 1957 to the end of 1963. Scrapping started in 1964 and by the end of 1966 there were only 76 of the class available for work. In 1966 a further heavy cull of these engines reduced their number to 23 and the last engine withdrawn was No 73069 in August 1968.

A total of 17 scrapyards and 2 BR locomotive works (Eastleigh 2 locos cut and Swindon 1 loco cut) took part in the scrapping of 167 engines and tenders, and that figure represented the eventual recycling of a little over 21 thousand tons of scrap metal. The biggest allocation of the class for cutting went to the South Wales yards of Cashmores at Great Bridge and Newport, who between them received 98 withdrawn members of the class. Scottish allocated locos were in the main cut at scrapyards north of the border and noticeably Motherwell Machinery & Scrap of Wishaw cut 19 locos, whilst Campbells of Airdrie disposed of 9 engines.

Preserved BR Standard Class 5 No 73096 is pictured heading a demonstration goods train at the Mid Hants Railway, during the occasion of a photographic charter on 16 January 2010. *Paul Pettitt*

The class leader No 73000 is pictured leaving Perth with an Aberdeen – Glasgow express on 18 September 1965. *David Anderson*

The preserved Caprotti locomotive No 73129 powers up the bank at Burrs, East Lancashire Railway whilst working from Heywood to Rawtenstall on 25 October 2010. *Fred Kerr*

Preserved BR Standard Class 5 No 73050 CITY OF PETERBOROUGH is pictured at Orton Mere on the Nene Valley Railway. The engine crew are collecting the single line token for the section to Wansford from the signaller, 22 September 1984. *Fred Kerr*

BR Standard Class 5 No 73047 on the now defunct Somerset & Dorset route at Devonshire Bank with a Bath–Templecombe local service in October 1963. *Authors Collection*

BR Standard Class 5 No 73062 is pictured at Kingsknowe with the 6.14pm Edinburgh–Glasgow service. The Caledonian Railway type Semaphore Route Indicator can just be seen in the centre of the buffer beam. *David Anderson*

Preserved BR Standard Class 5 No 73096 is seen passing Northwood Lane with the 12 noon Kidderminster–Bridgnorth service during a September 2003 visit to the Severn Valley Railway. *Fred Kerr*

BR Standard Class 5 No 73109 is pictured piloting Thompson Class B1 No 61219 past Haymarket Central Junction with a morning Glasgow Queen Street to Edinburgh Waverley train during September 1964. *David Anderson*

Preserved BR Standard Class 5 No 73129 is pictured in action at the East Lancashire Railway; the train is departing from Ramsbottom with a service for Rawtenstall on 25 October 2010. *Fred Kerr*

Scottish allocated BR Standard Class 5 on Beattock Bank, loco No 73076 was pictured with a London Euston–Perth service on 15 August 1955. *David Anderson*

Preserved BR Standard locomotives in action, 'Class 5' 4-6-0 No 73129 whilst in charge of a passenger service, passes Standard 'Class 4' 2-6-4 tank No 80002 which is shunting at Oxenhope on the Keighley & Worth Valley on 9 October 2010. Both engines were built by BR at Derby Works. *Fred Kerr*

BR Standard Class 5 No 73055 is pictured at Lamington on the WCML whilst in charge of the morning Carlisle–Glasgow stopping passenger train, 5 July 1958. *David Anderson*

Chapter 4

BR STANDARD 'CLASS 4MT' 4-6-0

The BR Standard Class 5 locomotives were rightly described as being reliable and popular with engine crews. However the BR Standard 4-6-0 '4MT' class of engines, which were built over the same time scale, were possibly received with even more enthusiasm by motive power depot staff. The '75000' concept envisaged a lightweight but reliable engine with wider route availability than the BR Standard Class 5 locos. In service the BR Class 4MT 4-6-0 tender engines quickly earned a reputation for reliability and also became known as the ultimate 'go anywhere' locomotives.

In particular on the BR Western Region, and by virtue of their 'L1' loading gauge status, they were allowed to work over many routes which even the '7800 Manor'

There were 80 of these locomotives built at Swindon Works between 1951 and 1957, and 6 of the class survived into preservation. Preserved loco No 75027 is pictured hard at work on the Bluebell Railway. *Paul Pettitt*

class engines were prohibited from using. That being because of another plus, the Standard 4's reduced width (compared to the Manors) allowed them to use routes which the Manors were additionally prohibited from using because of their excessive width 'over cylinders'. The maximum axle loading of the 4MT's was designed to be 17 tons 5 cwt (GWR/BR Manor axle load 'Blue'- up to 17 tons 12cwts, BR Standard Class 5 axle load 18 ton).

The Fairburn designed LMS 2-6-4T was the locomotive class from which the 4MT Standard 4-6-0s were derived. The BR4 boiler used actually evolved from the aforementioned tank engine, however in the case of the Standard 4MT tender locos the boiler's barrel was lengthened by 9 inches. The tender engine option of course provided more fuel and water, thus making the class eminently useful for longer journeys and giving the class wide route availability (when coupled with BR2 and BR2A tenders). The later use by the BR Southern Region of higher capacity BR1B tenders with some of their allocation restricted those engines to the same route availability as the BR Standard Class 5 4-6-0's. Originally the locos were outshopped in BR lined black livery.

The original intention was to build greater numbers of the 4MT 4-6-0 engines and to that end BR placed an order with Swindon Works for further batch which

BR Standard 4MT 4-6-0 No 75007 is pictured in superb condition at Oxford (81F) its home shed on 16 June 1962. Note that the 4MT WR Passenger Green (unlined) liveried loco is still fitted with the original design 'I' section coupling rods, also a concertina type draught excluders between cab and the BR2 3500 gallon tender can clearly be seen in the folded back position. *David Anderson*

were allocated the numbers 75080–75089. Those locos were destined for the BR Eastern Region however the onset of dieselisation caused the order to be cancelled.

Modifications

As originally built the BR Class 4 4-6-0 locos were fitted with forged 'I' section coupling rods, however during later modifications the class received new plain section coupling rods. As with other standard class tender engine builds these locos were over time fitted with concertina type draught excluders between cab and tender.

BR Western Region allocated locos, 75003 (12/59), 75005 (01/1962), 75006 (12/60), 75008 (09/62), 75020 (1962), 75026 (07/62) and 75029 (05/57) were fitted with double blast pipes and chimneys on the dates indicated. The whole of the BR Southern Region allocation of the class (locos 75065–75079) were fitted with modified double blast pipes and chimneys on dates between October 1960 and November 1961.

The Western Region double chimneys (fitted after draughting tests at Swindon Works) were considered by many observers to be over tall and also rather ugly looking castings which certainly detracted from what they thought to be the previously clean and neat lines of those engines. The WR double chimney engines were then out shopped in fully lined BR Passenger Green livery, as indeed were other single chimney locomotives after later visits to the works.

BR WR allocated BR Standard 4MT 4-6-0 No 75003 is pictured 'on shed' at Yeovil (83E), this loco re-entered traffic with the so called 'ugly' WR design of chimney in December 1959. *Mike Stokes Collection*

Southern Region allocated BR Standard
4MT 4-6-0 No 75076 is pictured
between turns at Feltham (70B) in
March 1966. Note the Eastleigh
produced double chimney design.
Authors Collection

BR Standard Class 4MT 4-6-0 No 75076 is pictured approaching Waterloo station, London on 7 April 1957, before acquiring a double chimney (fitted June 1961). Note also the BR1B 4725 gallon flush sided tender and plain section coupling rods. *D.C. Ovenden/Colour Rail*

The Southern Region works at Eastleigh produced what many agreed was a much neater double blast pipe and chimney design for their allocation of the 4MT 4-6-0 engines. Those locomotives (with the larger BR1B tender) retained a lined black livery style. The general consensus was that the double blastpipe and chimney modification further improved the performance of what were already fine machines.

In traffic

The BR Standard 4MT 4-6-0 engines were extremely popular with footplate crews and motive power depot personnel in all of the regions to which they were allocated. In the BR London Midland Region the locos worked regularly over many of the ex Cambrian Railway routes and as in other regions the 4MT 4-6-0 tender types earned a justified reputation for reliability.

From this image it could be assumed that in this instance ashpan removal is causing the loco crew a problem. Taken at Feltham depot during the summer of 1966 it shows the fireman in the pit, crowbar to hand, whilst the driver looks to be offering some advice! *Authors Collection*

In all 6 members of the class made it into preservation No 75014 home base Paignton & Dartmouth Steam Railway, No 75027 home base Bluebell Railway, No 75029 North Yorkshire Moors Railway, No 75069 home base Severn Valley Railway, No 75078 home base Keighley & Worth Valley Railway and No 75079

Original tender type allocations

Loco numbers	Tender type	Coal Capacity	Water Capacity
75000–74049	BR2 inset	6 ton	3500 gallon
75050–75064	BR2A inset	6 ton	3500 gallon
75065–75079	BR1B flush sided	7 ton	4725 gallon

home base Mid-Hants Railway. All but No 75079 have steamed in preservation and additionally Nos 75014, 75029 and 75069 have all worked over routes on the national network. Loco No 75079 was in 2012 still under restoration. See also http://www.watercressline.co.uk/The-Works/Locos/20

Disposal

All 80 locos were in traffic by the end of 1957 and the class remained intact until the first of the class to be withdrawn, No 75067, was retired from BR SR service in October 1964 after less than 10 years in service. Between 1964 and the end of 1966 the number of the class in service reduced to 46 engines. At the end of 1967 there were 10 BR Standard Class 4MT 4-6-0s still working and the last engine of the class to be withdrawn was No 75048 from the BR London Midland Region in August 1968

Preserved BR Standard Class 4MT 4-6-0 No 75027 'on shed' at Sheffield Park, Bluebell Railway is evocatively pictured on 16 August 2009. Note the BR2 3500 gallon tender. *Paul Pettitt*

Preserved BR Standard Class 4MT 4-6-0 No 75079 is pictured 'stored out of use' at Eastleigh (then 70D) in March 1967 having been withdrawn by BR SR in November 1966. *Mike Stokes Collection*

BR Standard 4 MT 4-6-0 'Class 4' class facts

4-6-0 BR Standard 'Class 4' – 80 locomotives built

Introduced: 1951–1957

Designer: Riddles. Parent office for design Brighton

Company: British Railways

Weight: 69 ton 0 cwt

Tender: BR1B 50 ton 5 cwt, BR2 42 ton 3 cwt, BR 2A 42 ton 3 cwt

Driving Wheel: 5 foot 8 inches diameter

Boiler Pressure: 225 psi superheated

Cylinders: 18 inch diameter x 28 inch stroke

Tractive Effort: 25515lbf

Valve Gear: Walschaert piston valves

Standard Class 4 4-6-0 build details

Loco numbers	Build location	Year
75000–75009	Swindon	1951
75010–75019	Swindon	1951/52
75020–75029	Swindon	1952/53
75030–75049	Swindon	1953/54
75050–75064	Swindon	1955/56
75065–75079	Swindon	1956/57

Original locomotive regional allocations

London Midland Region

75010–75019, 75030–75049, 75050–75064

Southern Region

75065–75079

Western Region

75000–75009, 75020–75029

Pictured whilst receiving attention, at Feltham (70B), BR Standard Class 4 No 76076. *Authors Collection*

Sheffield Park engine shed on the preserved Bluebell Railway makes the perfect setting for BR Standard Class 4MT 4-6-0 No 75027 which is seen in the company of BR Standard 4MT 2-6-4T 80151 (temporarily masquerading as sister engine No 80017) and Ivatt 2MT 2-6-2 No 41312. *Paul Pettitt*

BR Standard Class 4MT 4-6-0 No 75069 is pictured approaching Hampton Loade from Bridgnorth whilst temporarily masquerading as sister loco NO 75009 during a Somerset & Dorset Joint Railway themed weekend at the Severn Valley Railway. *Keith Langston*

London Midland Region allocated BR Standard Class 4MT 4-6-0 No 75064 is seen on the outskirts of Swinton, Manchester in this 1958 image. *Mike Stokes Collection*

Southern Region allocated BR Class 4MT 4-6-0 No 75065 departs from London Waterloo station with a Bournemouth train on 11 August 1966. *Mike Stokes Collection*

Western Region allocated BR Class 4MT 4-6-0 No 75006, soon to be a Bristol Bath Road (82A) allocated loco, is pictured fresh from the works at Swindon on 14 October 1951. *K.C.H. Fairey/Colour Rail*

BR Standard 4MT 4-6-0 No 75069 (complete with BR 1B tender) is pictured languishing at Woodham Brothers scrapyard Barry, but rescue was at hand and the loco was moved to the Severn Valley Railway in 1974. *Keith Langston*

Although a Southern Region loco preserved BR Standard 4MT 4-6-0 No 75069 was back on familiar BR 4MT 4-6-0 territory when pictured on 'Cambrian Limited' duty during June 1991. *Keith Langston*

Chapter 5

BR STANDARD 'CLASS 4MT' 2-6-0 (MOGUL)

BR Standard 'Class 4MT' mogul No 76114 is pictured at Doncaster in ex works condition on 12 October 1957. This was the last of 2,223 steam locomotives to be built at Doncaster Works. Note that by this time in the construction of the class the preferred style of coupling rods had been changed from 'I' section to plain section. In addition sister engine No 76099 was the last of 1,840 steam locomotive to be built at Horwich Works. *K.C.H. Fairey/Colour Rail*

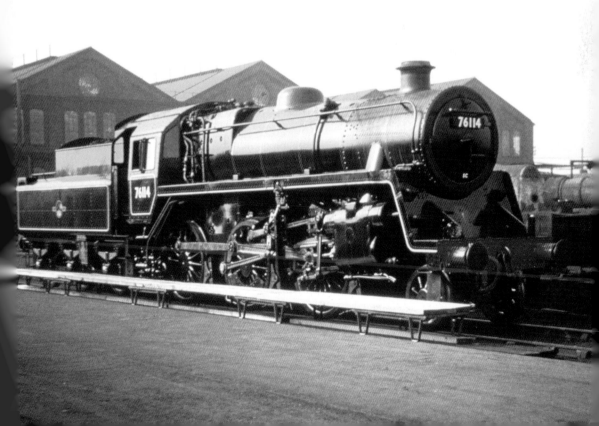

The BR Standard 4MT 2-6-0 class was in reality the 1947 LMS Ivatt 'Class 4' Mogul design modified to include BR Standard basic design features. The original class LMS Ivatt 2-6-0's were regarded as good strong locomotives however after tests at the Swindon Works test plant improvements in blastpipe and chimney construction were suggested and they were incorporated in the BR Standard 76000 class design. The selected boiler type was designated BR type 7.

With an axle-loading of only 16 tons 15 cwt the class was considered to be virtually unrestricted as to route availability. However use by the BR Southern Region of higher capacity BR1B tenders with their allocation somewhat restricted the route availability of those particular engines. In fact in those instances the axle loading of the tenders was greater than the engine. The choice of 5ft 3 inch diameter coupled wheels indicated that the designers intended the class to be used mainly on freight trains.

Most observers at the time were of the opinion that the standard engines were visually a much more pleasing design, as the 'Ivatt Moguls' were considered to be

Leader of the class No 76000 spent all of its working life allocated to Motherwell (66B) the loco is pictured on the turntable at Polmadie Glasgow (66A) in 1953. *Rail Photoprints Collection*

BR SR allocated BR Standard 'Class 4MT' mogul No 76062 is pictured between duties at Bournemouth Central on 28 June 1963, note the 71A (then Eastleigh) shedplate and BR1B flush sided tender. *Rail Photoprints Collection*

austere and basic in appearance. In particular the raised footplating of the Standard Mogul design was linked to the level of the buffer beam by a connecting sloping end section, which greatly tidied up the front end look of the locos. Originally the locos were outshopped in BR lined black livery. Batches were allocated to every BR region except the Western.

The BR Standard Class '4MT' Mogul type was in reality the 1947 LMS Ivatt Class 4MT' Mogul design modified to include BR Standard basic design features. Above, Preserved Ivatt Mogul No 43106 is pictured at Kidderminster on the Severn Valley Railway. Below, preserved BR Standard Class 4 Mogul No 76079 is seen in action at the Llangollen Railway. *Both images Keith Langston*

Modifications

In keeping with other BR Standard tender locomotive types the class were originally fitted with 'I' section coupling rods. On routine visits to the works of some locos, and during the construction of later models, the type of rods was changed to forged 'fish belly' plain section rods. As with other standard type tender engine builds these locos were overtime fitted with concertina type draught excluders between cab and tender.

In Traffic

The locos were well received by engine crews and motive power depot personnel and although designated as Mixed Traffic machines the Class 4 Standard Moguls were often to be seen on local passenger services. On the BR SR the original 37 allocated members of the class were initially concentrated in the area around Eastleigh, Southampton and Bournemouth. In addition to cross country passenger services they regularly worked the London Waterloo to Lymington boat train as they were included in a small number of modern tender engines which could use the turntable at Brockenhurst (loco and tender length over buffers 55 foot 10½ inches, wheelbase 46 foot 11¾ inches).

BR Standard Class 4 Mogul No 76037 is seen at Willesden shed (1A) in February 1965. Note that the concertina type draught excluder between cab and tender can be seen in the folded back position, and that the loco has plain section coupling rods. *Keith Langston*

Original tender type allocations

Loco numbers	Tender type	Coal Capacity	Water Capacity
76000–76044	BR2 inset	6 ton	3500 gallon
76045–76069	BR1B flush sided	7 ton	4725 gallon
76070–75114	BR2A inset	6 ton	3500 gallon

On 23 September 1954 while working the 7:00am Banbury to Eastleigh goods train locomotive No 76017 ran through a set of catch points and fell down an adjacent embankment. Fortunately no one was hurt and the loco was subsequently rescued by the Eastleigh and Fratton depot cranes, the loco was repaired and returned to service.

When the 35 strong batch of new engines first arrived at Scottish depots several of them were regularly used over the Waverley Route, between Carlisle and Hawick whilst other members of the class were to be seen on the famous 'Port Road' from Dumfries to Stranraer. The NE Region's contingent of 13 engines was widely spread around that territory and they particularly suited the severely weight restricted Stainmore Route. The BR ER initially divided its new 15 loco allocation between Stratford and Neasden. Of the BR LMR allocation all but two engines spent their working lives in the North West of England.

BR Standard Class 4 Mogul No 76039 is pictured 'on shed' at Neasden (then 34E) in 1955. Note that the loco has plain section coupling rods and a BR2 tender. *Rail Photoprints Collection*

Preserved BR Standard Class 4 Mogul No 76079 is seen dramatically approaching Buxton with a Dalesman charter train working whilst double heading with preserved Stanier Black Five 4-6-0 No 45407. *David Gibson*

In all 4 members of the class made it into preservation, No 76017 home base the Mid-Hants Railway, No 76077 home base the Gloucester & Warwickshire Railway, No 76079 home base North Yorkshire Moors Railway and No 76084 which is located at a private site in Morpeth, Northumberland. In 2012 locomotive No 76079 was the only member of the class which had been restored to working order. The loco has worked extensively at preserved railways and on the main line network. See also www.standard4.com , www.watercressline.co.uk , www.gwsr.com

Disposal

All 115 locos were in traffic by the end of 1957 and the class remained intact until No 76028 was withdrawn from BR SR service in May 1964. Between the end of 1963 and the end of 1966 the number of the class in service was further reduced to 40 engines. None of the class survived beyond the end of 1967 and the last to be withdrawn was No 76084 (preserved example) which was retired by BR LMR in November 1967.

BR Standard Class 4 Mogul No 76076 is pictured approaching Newton le Willows with a lengthy freight train on a wet day in 1963. *Colin Whitfield/Rail Photoprints Collection*

BR Standard 4 MT 2-6-0 (Mogul) 'Class 4' class facts

2-6-0 BR Standard 'Class 4' – 115 locomotives built

Introduced: 1952–1957

Designer: Riddles. Parent office for design Doncaster

Company: British Railways

Weight: 59 ton 2 cwt

Tender: BR1B 50 ton 5 cwt, BR2 42 ton 3 cwt, BR 2A 42 ton 3 cwt

Driving Wheel: 5 foot 3 inches diameter

Boiler Pressure: 225 psi superheated

Cylinders: 17 ½ inch diameter x 26 inch stroke

Tractive Effort: 24170lbf

Valve Gear: Walschaert piston valves

Southern Region allocated BR Standard 4MT Mogul No 76067 on shed at Basingstoke (formerly 70D) in June 1965. Interestingly the Basingstoke shed was officially closed by British Railways in 1963 but nevertheless stayed in use as a locomotive servicing point until the end of steam on the Southern Region (1967). Note the BR1B tender.
Brian Robbins/Rail Photoprints Collection

Standard Class 4 2-6-0 build details

Loco numbers	Build location	Year
76000–76004	Horwich	1952
76005–76019	Horwich	1952/53
76020–76024	Doncaster	1952/53
76025–76029	Doncaster	1953
76030–76044	Doncaster	1953/54
76045–76069	Doncaster	1955/56
76070–76074	Doncaster	1956
76075–76089	Horwich	1956/57
76090–76099	Horwich	1957
76100–76114	Doncaster	1957

Original locomotive regional allocations

Scottish Region

76000–76004, 76070–76074, 76090–76114

Southern Region

76005–76019, 76025–76029, 76053–76069

North Eastern Region

76020–76024, 76045–76052

Eastern Region

76030–76044

London Midland Region

76079-76089

Working over the long lamented S&DJR, BR Standard Class 4 Mogul No 76025 waits to depart from Radstock station with a Bournemouth West-Temple Meads train in October 1963. *Colour Rail*

BR Standard Class 4 Mogul No 76064 is pictured at work west of Woking with a down Ocean Liner Express working (regular boat train service between London and Southampton) on 1 July 1967. *David Rostance/Rail Photoprints Collection*

The beginning of 2004 saw BR Standard '4MT' 2-6-0 No 76079 hard at work piloting Class 7P6F No 34067 TANGMERE The preserved locomotives were approaching Copy Pit summit whilst working the Manchester–Morecambe stage of a rail tour which originated in Northampton, note that even though the pair are miles away from the location of the now closed Somerset & Dorset Joint Railway (S&JDR) the Standard Mogul still proudly carries a Pines Express headboard. *Fred Kerr*

Preserved BR Standard Class 4 Mogul No 76079 seen arriving at Glyndyfrdwy on the Llangollen Railway with the former Berwyn Belle dining train, the locos first owner in preservation Derek Foster is seen in charge. The BR2A tender can be clearly seen, these tenders, unlike the BR2 types, had a hinged fall plate bridging the tender and loco footplate. During its spell at Llangollen this loco carried the name Castel Dinas Bran, in celebration of a medieval castle the remains of which stand on a hill above the town of Llangollen. *Keith Langston*

BR Standard Class 4 Mogul No 76017, a preserved member of the class was at that time allocated to Salisbury (then 70E) the Class 4MT Mogul is pictured shunting stock at Axminster in the mid 1960s. The tender is a BR2 type, without fall plate. Note also the cab side triangle (yellow) denoting a Standard type loco equipped with French TIA water softening apparatus, which was originally identified by the way of a yellow spot painted just below the cab side number. However the spot was later changed to a triangle, in order to avoid confusion with the relevant Western Region (ex GWR) route availability code. Of further interest is the two disk Southern Region code on the tender which does not indicate the route being used and may have been left in position following a previous tender first working of a Bournemouth Central – Dorchester goods train. *David Anderson*

Blasting up the bank with a 7 coach train! BR Standard 4MT 2-6-0 No 76038 and an unidentified sister loco east bound on Talerddig between Machynlleth and Newtown in July 1966, the lead loco was withdrawn in September 1966. Note that the lead loco is minus a smokebox numberplate but has white painted door brackets and buffers. With a 700 plus feet summit, Talerddig presented a challenge to railway operators especially during wet conditions, in steam days heavy trains often required an assisting engine. A.E. Durant/Rail Photoprints Collection

BR Standard 4MT 2-6-0 No 76009 struggles up to Wolverhampton High Level with a substantial southbound freight on 17 July 1965. The train engine is being assisted on the rear by ex Midland Railway Jinty 0-6-0T No 47437. *Brian Robbins/Rail Photoprints Collection*

Preserved BR Standard Class 4MT Mogul No 76079 (complete with Pines Express headboard) leads Ivatt Moguls No 46443 and No 46521 through the delightfully period setting of Hampton Loade station, Severn Valley Railway with a triple light engine move during a September gala event. *Keith Langston*

Chapter 6

BR STANDARD 'CLASS 3MT' 2-6-0 (MOGUL)

The 1954 introduction of the class coincided with the completion of several British Railways civil engineering projects to upgrade many of the subsidiary lines for the use on which this class was designed. That fact together with the ever increasing introduction of Diesel Multiple Units (DMUs) quickly reduced the need for, and therefore the usefulness of, the BR Standard Class 3 MT Mogul

Scottish allocated BR Standard 3MT Mogul No 77015 is pictured at Kilmarnock station on 20 August 1960. *K.C.H. Fairey/Colour Rail*

tender type. As a direct result of which an order placed with Swindon to construct another 5 members of the class was cancelled.

This Standard Class 3MT 2-6-0 design was basically a tender version of the '82000' 3MT tank locomotive class. The Ivatt Mogul boiler was too heavy for both of those Standard locomotive designs, although it was dimensionally suitable. The chosen boiler was based on the proven Swindon No 4 design which was modified to suit BR Standard requirements. Those modifications included shortening the boiler barrel by a little over 5 inches and adding a dome, to what was originally a domeless unit when used with the GWR '5100', '5600' and '8100' classes. In addition the modified Swindon No 4 boilers, as fitted to the aforementioned Standard classes were fitted with an 18 element superheater in place of the original GWR Swindon 7 element specification.

Original tender type allocations

Loco numbers	Tender type	Coal Capacity	Water Capacity
77000–77019	BR2A inset	6 ton	3500 gallon

In Traffic

The Swindon built Class 3 BR Standard 2-6-0s operated mainly in the two regions to which they were allocated (Scottish and North Eastern). Notable exceptions were locos No 77011 and No 77014 which found their way south as they were both

BR Standard 3MT Mogul No 77003 is pictured double heading with BR Standard Class 4MT Mogul No 76049 whilst working the 9 coach RCTS 'Stainmore Limited' charter of 20 January 1962 (1X76 throughout) the location is Kirkby Stephen during the outward stop. This was the final day of operation of the Stainmore line, the route made famous by the British Transport Films classic offering 'Snowdrift at Bleath Ghyll'. *Colour Rail*

BR Standard 3MT Mogul No 77009 is pictured on shed at Polmadie Glasgow (66A) in the company of BR Standard 'Clan' No 72002, 27 July 1955. Note that the loco was fitted with flat section coupling rods and 'I' section driving rods. *David Anderson*

Scottish allocated BR Standard Class 3MT 2-6-0 No 77007 pictured during servicing at Polmadie (66A) on 28 August 1961. *K.C.H. Fairey/Colour Rail*

allocated to Northwich (then 8E formerly 9G) in the mid 1960s. Loco No 77011 was withdrawn from that depot in February 1966 whilst sister Loco No 77014 then ventured even further south being reallocated to Guildford (70C) from where it was later withdrawn.

Unfortunately no member of the class survived into preservation. With the benefit of hindsight it could be said that modern day preserved railways would find locomotives of this weight and power rating extremely useful additions to their available steam stock.

Disposal

All 20 locos were in traffic by the end of 1954 and the class remained intact until No 77010 (entered service June 1954) was withdrawn from BR North Eastern Region service in November 1965, serving BR for only 11 years and 4 months. By the end of 1966 the number of the class in service had been further reduced to only 3 engines. None of the class survived beyond the end of 1967 and the last to be withdrawn was No 77014, which was retired by BR Southern Region in July 1967.

BR Standard Class 3MT 2-6-0 No 77010 was a long way from its intended home territory when photographed at Bristol on 15 June 1954. As the loco officially entered BR service in June 1954 it can be assumed that this visit was part of a 'running in' trip from Swindon Works. Note the footplate crew member on top of the BR2A tender 'trimming the coal'. *Colour Rail*

BR Standard Class 3MT 2-6-0 No 77012 was attracting the attention of enthusiasts during a stop at Eaglescliffe in September 1955. *Keith Langston Collection*

BR Standard 4 MT 2-6-0 (Mogul) 'Class 4' class facts

2-6-0 BR Standard 'Class 3' 20 locomotives built

Introduced: 1952-1957
Designer: Riddles. Parent office for design Swindon
Company: British Railways
Weight: 57 ton 2 cwt
Tender: BR 2A 42 ton 3 cwt
Driving Wheel: 5 foot 3 inches diameter
Boiler Pressure: 200 psi superheated
Cylinders: 17 ½ inch diameter x 26 inch stroke
Tractive Effort: 21490lbf
Valve Gear: Walschaert piston valves

Standard Class 4 2-6-0 build details

Loco numbers	Build location	Year
77000–77019	Swindon	1954

Original locomotive regional allocations

North Eastern Region

77000–77004, 77010–77014

Scottish Region

77005–77009, 77015–77019

BR Standard Class 3MT 206-0 No 77004 was pictured setting back on to an infrastructure train at Stourton Yard, Leeds on 3 September 1966. *Mike Stokes Collection*

The prototype BR Standard Class 3MT 2-6-0 No 77000 pictured in light steam at its home depot of Hull Botanic Gardens (53B) circa 1956. *Rail Photoprints Collection*

Brand new BR Standard Class 3MT 2-6-0 No 77011 awaits transfer from Swindon Works in June 1954 to its first allocated shed which was Darlington (51A). *Rail Photoprints Collection*

Chapter 7

BR STANDARD 'CLASS 2MT' 2-6-0 (MOGUL)

BR Standard Class 2MT 2-6-0 No 78063 is pictured at Camden (1B) in September 1963. The loco is in a poor external condition with heat blistering evident to the smoke box paint. Like other BR Standard types the 2MT Moguls 'as built' were fitted with 'I' section coupling rods, many of which were later changed to flat section rods, as can clearly be seen is the case with No 78063. *Rail Photoprints Collection*

The BR Standard design team simply took the successful LMS Ivatt Class 2MT Mogul design of 1946 and modified it to comply with standard design criteria when creating this 'wide route availability' class of engines. The LMS Ivatt Mogul had proved itself to both reliable in service and economical in operation, in fact so much so that other regions placed orders for the Ivatt locos during the early period of nationalisation, in 1948 BR took into stock 128 Ivatt 2-6-0 engines.

The chosen boiler for the Standard Class 2 locomotives was designated as type BR8 and carried BR clack valve arrangement in place of the LMS top feed and additionally a sturdy looking standard type chimney. Observers at the time were of the opinion that the BR Class 2 was a much neater looking engine than its Ivatt predecessor. The loco's cab was given a much smoother look and was matched perfectly with the tender cab of the selected BR3 tender. The front end was neater than that of the original, it having a short drop plate ahead of the cylinders, to the footplate at buffer beam level. The class earned the nickname 'Mickey Mouse'.

In comparison with the Ivatt (also nick named Mickey Mouse) had two 16 inch diameter x 24 inch stroke length outside cylinders whilst the Standard Class 2 Mogul was fitted with 16½ inch diameter x 24 inch stroke length cylinders, with the BR version having a greater tractive effort (Ivatt 17400lbf – Standard class 2

BR Standard 2MT Mogul No 78007 passes GWR Mogul No 6336 as it approaches Machynlleth with a local service, circa 1961. *Alan H. Bryant ARPS/Rail Photoprints Collection*

MT 18513lbf). The Ivatt Class 2 tender engine was complemented by a 2-6-2 tank loco version as was the BR Standard Class 2 tender engine, which could be directly compared to the BR Standard 2-6-2T 84000 series.

The majority of these locomotives received a BR Standard lined black livery however the Western Region allocated engines were later given an unlined BR Brunswick Green livery by Swindon Works.

In Traffic

Despite the design work carried out to improve the cab and tender interface some loco crews did complain that the footplate of the Standard 2MT was a very draughty place to be. Some depots also entered reports that the engines did not steam well, but that did not seem to be universally the case. Although being physically the smallest standard type the 2MT locos were generally regarded as strong sure footed engines by the BR crews.

The London Midland Region received the largest allocation of the class and the type was often to be seen hard at work on both local passenger and freight services in the North West of England. The Scottish allocation was widespread with at least

BR Standard 2MT Mogul No 78048 is pictured heading west with a former brake being used as a tool van and a rather delightful vintage inspectors' saloon. The location is Haymarket Central Junction and the line crossing above the loco was the former Caledonian route linking Edinburgh Princess Street and Leith North, note the Caley signal box, now long gone. *David Anderson*

one loco operating from the depot at Kittybrewster (61A) and others from the border region depot at Hawick (64G) in addition Bathgate (64F) and Motherwell (66B) were home to others of the class.

Then allocated to West Auckland (51F) as part of the Eastern and North Eastern Region allocation (and now a preserved loco) No 78018 was famously the engine rescued from the snowdrift in the British Transport Film 'Snowdrift at Bleath Gill' (that engine finishing its working life in the Shrewsbury area). The Western Region engines were prominent on services over the former Cambrian Route.

The introduction of the class into service coincided with the completion of several British Railways civil engineering projects to upgrade many of the subsidiary lines for the use on which this class was designed. That fact together with the ever increasing introduction of Diesel Multiple Units (DMUs) quickly reduced the need for, and therefore the usefulness of, the BR Standard Class 2 MT Mogul tender engines.

Fortunately four of the class survived into preservation, the 'Bleath Gill' loco No 78018 home base Darlington Railway Preservation Society, No 78019 home base Great Central Railway, No 78022 home base Keighley & Worth Valley Railway. Loco No 78018 is still under restoration whilst Nos 78019 and 78022 have both steamed in preservation. Loco No 78059 was saved for preservation but was minus its tender which had been cut for scrap, interestingly this engine in 2012 was being rebuilt as BR Standard Class tank loco No 84030 at the Bluebell Railway. See also www.drps.synthasite.com www.bluebellrailway.co.uk/bluebell/locos/84030

BR Western Region allocated Standard 2MT Mogul No 78006 is pictured whilst pausing at Barmouth (ex Cambrian Route) with a north bound local service, circa 1962. Note that the Machynlleth (89C) driver has chosen the occasion to hold up the platform lighting column! The train would probably be waiting to pass a southbound service. *Alan H. Bryant ARPS/Rail Photoprints Collection*

BR Western Region allocated Standard 2MT Mogul No 78007 is seen outside Swindon Works circa 1960, note the original design 'I' section coupling rods. *Keith Langston Collection*

Disposal

All 65 locos were in traffic by the end of 1956 and the class remained intact until No 78015 was withdrawn from BR North Eastern Region service in November 1963, after only 9 years 7 months in traffic. Between the end of 1963 and the end of 1966 the number of the class in service was further reduced to 12 engines. None of the class survived beyond May 1967 when No 78062 (the last to be withdrawn) was retired by BR LMR.

Original tender type allocations

Loco numbers	Tender type	Coal Capacity	Water Capacity
78000–78064	BR3 inset	4 ton	3000 gallon

Standard 2MT Mogul No 78019 pictured hard at work during a September 2009 visit to the Llangollen Railway. *Fred Kerr*

Design comparison. Above preserved Ivatt Class 2MT 2-6-0 No 46441 is pictured on Crewe Works during the occasion of the 2004 Great Gathering event. Below BR Standard 2MT 2-6-0 No 78003 was pictured at Bangor (6H) in May 1963. *Both pictures Keith Langston*

BR Standard 2 MT 2-6-0 (Mogul) 'Class 2' class facts

2-6-0 BR Standard 'Class 2' - 65 locomotives built

Introduced: 1953-1956

Designer: Riddles. Parent office for design Derby

Company: British Railways

Weight: 49 ton 5 cwt

Tender: BR3 36 ton 17 cwt

Driving Wheel: 5 foot diameter

Boiler Pressure: 200 psi superheated

Cylinders: 16 ½ inch diameter x 24 inch stroke

Tractive Effort: 18515lbf

Valve Gear: Walschaert piston valves

Standard Class 4 2-6-0 build details

Loco numbers	Build location	Year
78000–78009	Darlington	1952/53
78010–78019	Darlington	1953/54
78020–78044	Darlington	1954
78045–78054	Darlington	1954
78055–78064	Darlington	1956

Preserved BR Standard 2MT 2-6-0 No 78019 looked to be in excellent working order passing Hambleton Bridge during a photographic charter on the Embsay & Bolton Abbey Steam Railway during September 2009. *Fred Kerr*

Now preserved BR Standard 2MT 2-6-0 No 78022 pictured whilst hard at work for British Railways, the year was 1964 and the location is Preston. *Keith Langston*

BR Standard 2MT 2-6-0 No 78022 pictured at the East Lancashire Railway, note the scorched smokebox door, an effect usually caused by the build up of hot ash. *Keith Langston*

BR Standard 2MT 2-6-0 No 78055 runs through the north end of Crewe station light engine, February 1962. *Rail Photoprints Collection*

BR Standard 2MT 2-6-0 No 78064 stands in a bay platform at the south end of Crewe station, circa 1959. Note the 27D (Wigan Central L&Y) shedplate. *Alan H. Bryant ARPS/Rail Photoprints Collection*

BR Standard 2MT 2-6-0 No 78063 on shed at Willesden (1A) in February 1965. Note the flat section coupling rods and speedo connection. *Keith Langston*

Preserved loco No 78019 is pictured whilst receiving attention at the works of LNWR Heritage Ltd Crewe, loco fitter Mark O'Brien is seen replacing boiler tubes. *Keith Langston*

BR Standard 2MT 2-6-0 No 78030 on shed at Crewe North (5A), March 1965. *Keith Langston Collection*

BR Standard 2MT 2-6-0 No 78021 is seen outside Crewe works in August 1955. *Keith Langston Collection*

Preserved BR Standard 2MT 2-6-0 No 78019 is seen passing Llangollen Canal and heading towards the Dee Bridge on the Llangollen Railway, 20 April 2007. *Fred Kerr*

Chapter 8

BR STANDARD 'CLASS 4MT' 2-6-4T 'CLASS 4 TANK'

Preserved BR Standard Class 4MT 2-6-4T No 80151 makes a fine sight rounding the curve at Monteswood Lane on the Bluebell Railway, 21 February 2009. *Paul Pettitt*

The Fairburn LMS 2-6-4t design of 1945, which had been developed from a 1935 Stanier 2 cylinder design, was at first considered for inclusion in the Standard range of engines, albeit in a slightly modified form. However as the design team wished to incorporate features which would allow the class to comply with the ruling 'L1' loading gauge more substantial alterations were specified. The Fairburn boiler design was altered to comply with the loading gauge requirements and also incorporate standard design features. Boiler clack feed valves of a Southern pattern were used in place of the LMS top feed with the regulator rodding to the dome running externally from the cab.

The aforementioned LMS tank locomotives were built with cylinders of $19^5/8$ inches diameter and a stroke length of 26 inches. For the new design to comply with the 'LI' loading gauge the cylinders had to no more that 18 inch in diameter. The LMS Fairburn locos operated with a boiler pressure of 200psi but in order to gain the required tractive effort the Standard 4MT 2-6-4 engines were designed to operate at 225 psi. Piston stroke length was set at 28 inch and the tractive effort was raised to 25,515ldf (Fairburn 2-6-4T 24,670lbf). The BR Standard Class 4MT 4-6-0 was basically a tender engine derivative of this 2-6-4 tank loco.

Another 15 of the class were on order to be constructed in 1957; however rapidly increasing dieselization caused that order to be cancelled. In fact had the last five

BR Standard Class 4MT 2-6-4T No 80030 was pictured at Glasgow Corkerhill (67A) depot in 1952, the proud driver poses with the then 'new' loco whilst his fireman looks on from the cab window. This loco has 'I' section coupling rods. *Rail Photoprints Collection*

locos being built at Brighton (Nos 80150 – 80154) not been at such an advanced stage of construction their build would also have been cancelled by the BR board.

Modifications

No significant modifications to the basic design were made during the working lives of the class. However the water tank air vent was found to partially restrict the driver's forward vision and as a consequence it was moved further forward from the build of No 80059 onward. As had been the case with other BR Standard types the original 'I' section (fluted) coupling rods were considered to be problematic and from the build of No 80079 the specification was changed to include plain section rods.

The chosen livery for the class was BR lined black.

In Traffic

Like their Stanier/Fairburn 4MT 2-6-4T predecessors the BR Standard Class 4MT 2-6-4Ts proved to be extremely popular with locomotive crews and had a good turn of speed with more than adequate powers of acceleration. Equally at home working freight or passenger services the type were originally allocated to all BR regions with the exception of the Western. However as steam was displaced by

BR Standard Class 4MT 2-6-4T No 80012 approaches Victoria with a service from Tunbridge Wells West, on 21 May 1952. *C. R. L. Coles/Rail Photoprints Collection*

electrified and diesel services in the south of England a batch of the 4MT tanks were sent to the BR Western Region.

On the BR Southern Region the class became associated with commuter trains out of London and running over the former London, Tilbury & Southend Line (LT&S) until the electrification of that route was completed in 1962. The un-electrified portions of the former London, Brighton & South Coast Railway (LB&SCR) were also extensively worked by the class. Scottish allocated examples were to be seen at work in the Glasgow area on commuter services and in particular on services along the coastal route to Greenock and Gourock.

The locomotives later transferred to the BR Western Region (Cardiff East Dock 88B) were well received by crews working valley line services. Reportedly they were also found to be ideal motive power for the Central Wales Line. London Midland Region depots with original allocations of the class included Watford (1C), Bletchley (4A) Bedford (15D) where the locos were gainfully employed on commuter services. Depots in the Eastern Region with allocations of the class included Plaistow (33A), Neasden (34E/14D) and York (50A) where they worked commuter services and local passenger trains.

As stated the 4MT Standard tank locomotives proved to be very popular in BR service, an opinion obviously echoed by the preservation movement as

Almost new BR Standard Class 4MT 2-6-4T No 80028 stands on the turntable at Kittybrewster depot (61A), in January1952. *Rail Photoprints Collection*

Number	In Traffic	Builder	Ex BR	Home Base
80002*	October 1952	Derby	March 1967	Keighley & Worth Valley Railway
80064	June 1953	Brighton	September 1965	Bluebell Railway
80072	November 1963	Brighton	July 1965	Llangollen Railway
80078	February 1954	Brighton	July 1965	Swanage Railway
80079	March 1954	Brighton	July 1965	Severn Valley Railway
80080	March 1954	Brighton	July 1965	Midland Railway Butterley
80097	December 1954	Brighton	July 1965	East Lancashire Railway
80098	December 1954	Brighton	July 1965	Midland Railway Butterley
80100	January 1955	Brighton	July 1965	Bluebell Railway
80104	March 1955	Brighton	July 1965	Swanage Railway
80105	April 1955	Brighton	July 1965	Bo'ness & Kinneil Railway
80135	April 1956	Brighton	July 1965	North Yorkshire Moors Railway
80136	May 1956	Brighton	July 1965	Churnet Valley Railway
80150	December 1956	Brighton	October 1965	Mid Hants Railway
80151	January 1957	Brighton	May 1967	Bluebell Railway

*Although officially withdrawn No 80002 reportedly remained in Glasgow past the end of steam haulage and was employed until 1969 on carriage heating duties.

15 examples (of the 155 strong class) have been saved. At the start of 2012 all but three of those (80097, 80100 and 80150) had been made operational again, restored examples have operated not only at preserved railways but additionally on the national network. See also www.80097.webs.com/locomotiveworkshop; www.bluebell-railway.co.uk/bluebell/pics/80100 and www.watercressline.co.uk

Disposal

All 155 locos were in traffic by the end of 1957 and the class remained intact until No 80103 was withdrawn from BR Eastern Region service in September 1962, after only 7 years 6 months in traffic. That loco was reported for rough riding by footplate crew and when examined at Stratford Works it was discovered that the mainframe was broken in half. Considered beyond economic repair No 80103 was withdrawn and scrapped. Between the end of 1963 and the end of 1964 the number

Above. BR Standard Class 4MT 2-6-4T No 80135 pictured at Plaistow (33A) in the company of sister loco No 80134, note that this loco has plain section coupling rods.

Below. LMS Fairburn 4MT 2-6-4T No 42289 pictured at Willesden (1A) also in the company of a sister loco. *Keith Langston Collection*

The Fairburn LMS 2-6-4t design of 1945, which had been developed from a 1935 Stanier 2 cylinder design, was at first considered for inclusion in the Standard range of engines, albeit in a slightly modified form. However the design team wished to incorporate other features in the new class of tank engines which would allow them to be compliant with the ruling loading gauge.

of the class in service was further reduced to 123 engines, the number was further reduced to 79 by the end of 1965. Some 25 of the class survived beyond the end of 1966. None of the class survived beyond July 1967 when No 80152 (the last to be withdrawn) was retired by BR Southern Region.

Original locomotive regional allocations

Scottish Region

80000–80009, 80020–80030, 80031–80033, 80054–80058, 80106–80115, 80121–80130

Southern Region

80010–80019, 80145–80154

London Midland Region

80034–80053, 80059–80068, 80081–80095

Eastern Region

80069–80080, 80096–80105, 80116–80120, 80131–80144

Whilst under restoration Llangollen Railway based BR Standard Class 4MT 2-6-4T No 80072 visited Crewe Works on the occasion of 'The Great Gathering' in 2004. The engine was pictured in the works erecting shop. *Keith Langston*

BR Standard 'Class 4MT' 2-6-4T 'Class 4 Tank' class facts

2-6-4T BR Standard 'Class 4 Tank' - 155 locomotives built

Introduced: 1951–1957

Designer: Riddles. Parent office for design Brighton

Company: British Railways

Weight: 88 ton 10 cwt

Tender Coal Capacity: 3½ ton

Water Capacity: 2000 gallons

Driving Wheel: 5 foot 8 inch diameter

Boiler Pressure: 225 psi superheated

Cylinders: 18 inch diameter x 28 inch stroke

Tractive Effort: 25515lbf

Valve Gear: Walschaert piston valves

Standard Class 4 2-6-4T build details

Loco numbers	Build location	Year
80000–80009	Derby	1951
80010–80019	Brighton	1951/52
80020–80033	Brighton	1952
80034–80053	Brighton	1952
80054–80058	Derby	1954/55
80059–80068	Brighton	1953
80069–80080	Brighton	1953/54
80081–80095	Brighton	1954
80096–80105	Brighton	1954/55
80106–80115	Doncaster	1954
80116–80120	Brighton	1955
80121–80130	Brighton	1955
80131–80144	Brighton	1956
80145–80154*	Brighton	1954/1956

*Loco No 80154 was the last of 1,211 steam locomotives to be built at Brighton Locomotive Works.

BR Standard Class 4MT 2-6-4T No 80002 is about to depart from Port Glasgow station with a local service to Gourock in July 1965. *John Vaughan/Rail Photoprints Collection*

Preserved BR Standard Class 4MT 2-6-4T No 80151 pictured on shed at Sheffield Park, Bluebell Railway in 2004. This loco was originally allocated to Brighton (75A) and was withdrawn by British Railways from Eastleigh (71A) in May 1967. *Paul Pettitt*

Fresh from the works, BR Standard Class 4MT 2-6-4T No 80022 (later destined to be a Glasgow Polmadie based loco) is pictured after a running in turn, December 1952. *Mike Stokes Collection*

Preserved BR Standard Class 4MT 2-6-4T No 80072 was rebuilt at the Llangollen Railway, which is now the Brighton built engines home base. The 'Class 4 Tank Standard' in partly rebuilt form is pictured on public display in the erecting shop at Crewe Works, during the occasion of the September 2004 Great Gathering. *Keith Langston*

On home territory, preserved BR Standard Class 4MT 2-6-4T No 80072 is seen during 'running in' and when making a smart getaway from Glyndyfrdwy with a train for Carrog. This loco was first allocated to Plaistow (33A) and withdrawn by British Railways from Shrewsbury (84G). *Keith Langston*

BR Standard Class 4MT 2-6-4T No 80109 is pictured at Balerno Junction with an Edinburgh (Princes Street) to Glasgow (Central) stopping train on 31 August 1957. Note the Caledonian Railway Semaphore Route Indicator on the buffer beam and the blue backed smokebox number and shed plate. *David Anderson*

Derby built preserved BR Standard Class 4MT 2-6-4T No 80002 is pictured at work whilst double heading with WD No 90733 at Oxenhope on the Keighley & Worth Valley Railway (the locos home base) in October 2010. This 4MT was withdrawn by British Railways in March 1967. *Fred Kerr*

BR Standard Class 4MT 2-6-4T No 80118 was pictured shunting Royal Mail vans at Glasgow Central station in October 1966. *Brian Robbins/Rail Photoprints Collection*

BR Standard Class 4MT 2-6-4T No 80064 is seen getting to grips with a heavy up freight train near Axminster in this 1960 image. *David Anderson*

BR Standard Class 4MT 2-6-4T No 80138 climbs away from Midford on the former Somerset & Dorset Joint Railway route with the 1.10 Bath Green Park–Templecombe service, 23 September 1965. *Rail Photoprints Collection*

BR Standard Class 4MT 2-6-4T No 80149 pauses at Bramber station whilst working a Brighton–Horsham service, the guard appears to be passing a 'note' to the driver, June 1960. *Dave Cobbe Collection–C. R. L. Coles/Rail Photoprints Collection*

Preserved BR Standard Class 4 Tanks in Snowdonia, locos No 80079 and No 80098 are pictured on the single line between Betws-y-Coed and Blaenau Ffestiniog in October 1999. *Keith Langston*

Severn Valley Railway based privately owned Preserved BR Standard Class 4MT 2-6-4T No 80079 is seen leaving Hampton Loade with a demonstration freight train working for Kidderminster. *Keith Langston*

BR Standard Class 4MT 2-6-4T No 80141 in the company of loco No 73170 stands 'stored out of use' at Nine Elms (70A), note that the coupling rods have been removed prior to moving for disposal. *Keith Langston*

Preserved BR Standard Class 4MT 2-6-4T No 80136 is pictured during a 2010 visit to the LNWR Heritage Ltd locomotive works at Crewe. This loco's home base is the Churnet Valley Railway. *Keith Langston*

Preserved BR Standard Class 4MT 2-6-4T No 80098 is seen Consall station on the Churnet Valley railway. This loco's home base is The Midland Railway Centre, Butterley. *David Gibson*

BR Standard 4MT 2-6-4 No 80145 was pictured whilst on station pilot duty outside London Waterloo. *Mike Stokes Collection*

BR Standard Class 4MT 2-6-4T No 80148 pictured outside the station at Brighton in August 1957. *Keith Langston*

Preserved Severn Valley Railway based BR Standard 4MT 2-6-4 No 80079, pictured on home territory shunting fright stock at Hampton Loade station, in 2009. *Keith Langston*

Loco No 80150, a candidate for restoration was pictured in 'Barry 10' condition at the Vale of Glamorgan Railway in 2010. *Keith Langston*

Preserved BR Standard Class 4MT 2-6-4T No 80079 is seen crossing the river Dee outside Chester whilst heading for Conway Climber duty in Snowdonia. *Keith Langston*

BR Standard Class 4MT 2-6-4T No 80080, which is now preserved, is pictured outside the shed at Oswestry (then 89D) just prior to being withdrawn by BR, note that the smokebox number plate is missing. *Mike Stokes Collection*

Preserved BR Standard 4MT -6-4 No 80098 is a regular visitor to heritage lines, the loco was pictured hard at work during a visit to the Churnet Valley Railway. *David Gibson*

Preserved BR Standard Class 4MT 2-6-4T locomotive No 80079 leads sister engine No 80098 into the setting sun and up the incline towards the tunnel and thereafter Blaenau Ffestiniog, whilst on Conway Climber duty, October 1999. *Keith Langston*

Chapter 9

BR STANDARD 'CLASS 3MT' 2-6-2T 'CLASS 3 TANK'

BR Standard 3MT 2-6-2T No 82041 doing a job it was built to do, hauling branch line and secondary route local passenger services. The Swindon built Class 3 Tank is seen at Bath Green Park station (former Somerset & Dorset Joint Railway) with a service for Bristol in April 1963. In 2012 the impressive station building survives as a civic amenity, but the railway alas is no more. *Rail Photoprints Collection*

The BR Standard Class 3 2-6-2T and its corresponding 2-6-0 tender engine Class 3 locomotives were designed with a specific purpose in mind. The BR network at that time included several regularly used routes which were restricted to locomotives with a maximum16 ton axle loading. The fact that some of the traffic on those routes required locomotives of a higher power rating than that of Class 2 engines highlighted the need for wide availability (low axle load) engines. The tender version naturally offered a greater operating range with coal capacity of 6 tons and water capacity of 3500 gallons against the tank engine Class 3 types which carried only 3 tons of coal and 1500 gallons of water.

Although the boiler used by the LMS Ivatt Mogul Class 4 locomotives was dimensionally suitable it was too heavy necessitating the Standard Design Team to look elsewhere. Their solution was to use the proven Swindon No 4 boiler as incorporated in the GWR 2-6-2T 51xx/81xx and the 56xx 0-6-2T engines. To comply with Standard practice, and accommodate design criteria, a dome was

BR Standard 3MT 2-6-2T No 82025 is pictured in the erecting shop at Swindon Works during construction, October 1954. *The 82045 Steam Locomotive Trust*

added to what had been originally a domeless boiler and the barrel was shortened by almost 6 inches. In addition there were some constructional changes and the Swindon 7 element superheater was replaced by one of an 18 element design. The new boiler was classified as type BR6.

Modifications

No significant modifications to the basic design were made during the working lives of the class. However later constructed members of the class had a slightly different boiler tube configuration and a larger-capacity coal bunker, in essence the self-trimming slope at the base of the original bunker was done away with in order to allow for an extra three quarters of a ton of coal.

As had been the case with other BR Standard types the original 'I' section (fluted) coupling rods were considered to be problematic and were changed to include plain section rods from the build of No 82020 onwards. The chosen livery for the class was BR lined black however Swindon (during general repair visits) painted some of the class in unlined BR Green (with large BR totem) whilst others were liveried in fully lined out BR Green. On some of the WR general repair works visits several locos were fitted with an extra small grab rail just ahead of the steam dome

BR Standard 3MT 2-6-2T No 82022 is seen at Exmouth station on 25 July 1956, and is about to depart with a train for Exeter. *David Anderson*

In Traffic

Although a successful design of engine the usefulness of the Class 3 2-6-2Ts was severely curtailed by both the rapid advancement of dieselisation and the upgrading of previously low axle loading sections of the permanent way. The 1954 British Railways steam locomotive building programme included a provision for a further two batches of the class to be built. Locomotives No 82045 to No 82054 were to be supplied to the BR Western Region and locomotives No 82055 to 82062 were intended for allocation to the BR North Eastern Region, both batches were to be constructed at Swindon Works, however the order was cancelled.

Disposal

All 45 locos were in traffic by the end of 1955 and the class remained intact until February 1964 when Nos 82002, 82008 and 82043 were withdrawn after a little under 12 years in traffic. Between the end of 1963 and the end of 1964 the number of the class in service was further reduced to 35 engines, the number was further reduced to 2 by the end of 1966. None of the class survived beyond July 1967 when No 82019 and No 82029 were retired by BR. None of the class survived into preservation however a 'new build' representative of the type was under construction in 2012.

BR Standard 3MT 2-6-2T No 82018 is pictured with a local stopping train approaching Tipton St Johns station. This station was closed under the Beeching cuts in 1967. First opened in 1874, it served as the junction for the Budleigh Salterton Railway. *David Anderson*

Surplus to requirements! BR Standard 3MT 2-6-2T No 82029 is pictured as withdrawn and before removal to Birds of Risca for 'cutting'. *The 82045 Steam Locomotive Trust*

BR Standard 'Class 3MT' 2-6-2T 'Class 3 Tank' class facts

2-6-2T BR Standard 'Class 3 Tank' - 45 locomotives built

Introduced: 1952-1955

Designer: Riddles. Parent office for design Swindon

Company: British Railways

Weight: 73 ton 10 cwt

Tender Coal Capacity: 3 ton

Water Capacity: 1500 gallons

Driving Wheel: 5 foot 3 inch diameter

Boiler Pressure: 200 psi superheated

Cylinders: 17½ inch diameter x 26 inch stroke

Tractive Effort: 21490lbf

Standard Class 3 2-6-2T build details

Loco numbers	Build location	Year
82000–82009	Swindon	1952
82010–82019	Swindon	1952
82020–82029	Swindon	1954
82030–82034	Swindon	1954/55
82035–82044	Swindon	1955

Original locomotive regional allocations

Western Region

82000–82009, 82030–82044

Southern Region

82010–82019, 82020–82029

BR Standard 3MT 2-6-2T No 82031 was pictured approaching Newton Abbott with a local service on 30 April 1955. *L.F. Folkard/Colour Rail*

BR Standard 3MT 2-6-2T No 82001 prepares to leave Highbridge for Evercreech Junction (former S&DJR) in September 1962. *Rail Photoprints Collection*

BR Standard 3MT 2-6-2T No 82041 is pictured 'on shed' and between turns at Bath S&D (82F). S&DJR Fowler 'Jinty' No 47465 can be glimpsed in the shed building. *Mike Stokes Collection*

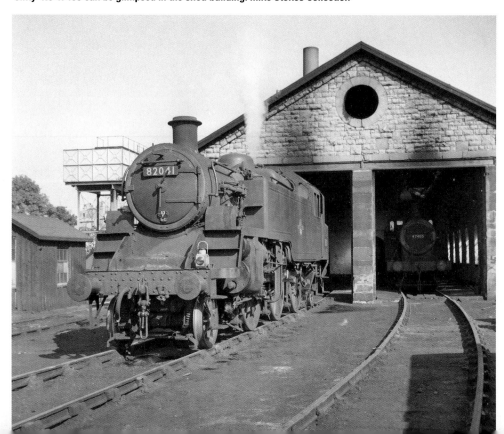

BR Standard 3MT 2-6-2T No 82005 passes GWR 0-6-0PT No 7405 as it leaves Barmouth for Machynlleth on the Cambrian route, circa 1962. The extra grab rail ahead of the dome (added at Swindon Works during a repair visit) can be seen in this image. *Alan H. Bryant ARPS/Rail Photoprints Collection*

BR Standard 3MT 2-6-2T No 82005 is again seen on the Cambrian this time after taking water and before departing from Porthmadog station in July 1962. *Alan H. Bryant ARPS/Rail Photoprints Collection*

Brand new BR Standard 3MT 2-6-2T No 82004 stands at Bristol Stapleton Road station whilst on a 'running in' turn from Swindon Works, 17 May 1952. As originally built the extra grab rail ahead of the steam dome was not fitted. *R. S. Wilkins/Rail Photoprints Collection*

BR Standard 3MT 2-6-2T No 82024 is pictured between duties at Exmouth Junction (then 72A) on 7 June 1955. *David Anderson*

BR Standard 3MT 2-6-2T No 82038 is pictured whilst leaving the old terminus at Bristol Temple Meads with a service for Bath Green Park, 7 July 1965, note the mainline Brush diesel on the centre road. *John Chalcraft/ Rail Photoprints Collection*

BR Standard 3MT 2-6-2T No 82029 is seen at the buffer stops, after working an ECS train into Waterloo station in 1965. *Brian Robbins/Rail Photoprints Collection*

BR Standard 3MT 2-6-2T No 82013 is seen between duties at London Waterloo station in 1963. *Mike Stokes Collection*

Originally a BR Western Region allocated engine BR Standard 3MT 2-6-2T No 82006 working as station pilot at Waterloo on the BR Southern Region in 1964, note also the departing SR Bulleid 'West Country' Pacific No 34006 Bude. *Mike Stokes Collection*

The '82045 Steam Locomotive Trust' –
New Build Locomotive

As 2012 dawned a group of dedicated enthusiasts were continuing to raise funds for, and actively constructing, what will effectively become the 46th member of the BR Standard 3MT 2-6-2T class of locomotives. The initial idea to build the 3MT 2-6-2T came from Paignton based South Devon Railway Railway (SDR) fireman John Besley in the 1990s. Thereafter, because of John's work and family commitments Severn Valley Railway (SVR) enginemen Tony Massau and Chris Proudfoot took up the challenge. The project was kick started in 2003 and then really took off when the Bridgnorth locomotive works of the SVR was later chosen as a manufacturing base.

BR Standard 3MT 2-6-2T No 82045, in ex-Works condition. *Artist Jonathan Clay.*

The 82000 3MT 2-6-2T class were the only BR Standard tank locomotives to carry more than one livery. Although all of them were originally turned out in lined black, those examples that worked on the Western Region were repainted in green after overhaul. The engines looked equally smart lined out in either livery, rather less so in the unlined green carried latterly by a number of examples.

As loco No 82045 was destined for the British Railways Western Region (had it been built as planned in 1956) it has been decided that the finished loco should appear in the attractive Swindon-inspired livery of BR Dark Green, lined out in orange and black. A later repaint into lined black could be an option.

The groups Bridgnorth HQ took delivery of a set of finished frame plates for the new engine in the autumn of 2008, a great step forward. Despite three bad winters in a row progress on the construction of this, a most practical type of new-build locomotive has been fairly rapid. There is still a long way to go before No 82045 steams in traffic but potential and existing supporters could in 2012 perceive the ongoing progress for themselves.

The Riddles Class 3 2-6-2 tanks, and their mogul sisters in the 77000 class all somehow slipped through the 1960s preservation net, and all went to the scrapyards. Three of the tanks did however survive in their allocated scrapyards until October 1968 and as such were prime candidates for preservation. Unfortunately no member/s of the then burgeoning steam locomotive preservation movement came forward with any tangible rescue plan/s; accordingly those locos were also cut for scrap (No 82003 and No 82031 by Cashmores of Newport and No 82018 by Buttigiegs of Newport). The new build group have decided to redress the balance and with the benefit of hindsight they rightly claim that these smart little engines would have been ideally suited to conditions on today's heritage railway lines. When completed loco No 82045 will doubtless prove them right.

The locomotive frames are pictured after the addition of the smoke box saddle on 31 November 2011. Proof, if indeed proof were needed that the 82045 tank locomotive project is well underway. *The 82045 Steam Locomotive Trust*

The 82045 Locomotive Fund, as the group was initially called, was re-constituted as a company limited by guarantee in April 2009 and gained charitable status in January of the following year. This was accompanied by a change of name to 'The 82045 Steam Locomotive Trust', whose stated aim is to build the next member of the extinct Riddles class (the BR engines finished at 82044) specifically for heritage line use and with no plans to run on the main line unless, of course, a potential benefactor wishes to see this happen and is prepared to put up the cash for it.

The Trust is entirely independent and self-financing though based on the Severn Valley, and the intention is that 82045 will join the West Midlands line's steam fleet but will be available for hire to other heritage railways at the Trust's discretion and that of the SVR.

In January 2012 the engine's chassis was complete, all frame stretchers and horns fabricated and fitted and the impressive smokebox saddle mounted between the frames. The riveting of the frame assembly is to be undertaken by the SVR on a contract basis. The patterns for the motion brackets were being cast (by a contractor) and the Trust had placed the order for the cylinders (including pattern making) casting and machining.

Despite three bad winters in a row progress on the construction of this, a most practical type of new-build locomotive has been fairly rapid. In this spring 2010 image taken at the SVR the assembled main frames, including buffer beam are seen before the addition of the smokebox saddle. *The 82045 Steam Locomotive Trust*

The necessary finance for this major job was in hand, and accordingly the cylinder assemblies were expected to be completed during the later months of 2012. The Trust needs to continue fund raising in order to progress the project further. The next big item on their manufacturing agenda will be the casting of the locomotives 5 foot 3 inch diameter driving wheels for which the No 82045 builders already have a pattern.

The main fund raising focus at present is an appeal to finance the manufacture of the locomotives wheels. In all six driving wheels to be cast, machined (the Trust already has the pattern), tyred and pressed on to axles; plus the front and rear pony truck assemblies. The total cost of that work is estimated to be in the region of £150k. Under the terms associated with being a charitable trust the 82045 Steam Locomotive Trust is obliged to seek the most favourable quote for all such major work.

Locomotive No 82045, therefore, will emerge from Bridgnorth Works an identical locomotive (as far as this is still possible) to the one that should have been built by British Railways at Swindon early in 1956. The later members of the BR Riddles Class 3 2-6-2T class had a slightly different boiler tube configuration and an increased capacity coal bunker (the self-trimming slope at the base of the original bunker was done away with in order to allow for an extra three quarters of a ton of coal), and 82045 will reflect these minor changes.

New built locomotives, in keeping with all restoration projects have to tackle head on the perennial problem of cash flow. Estimated total cost of constructing No 82045 is expected to be of the order of about £1.25 million and the Trust had by 2012 raised some £150,000, a figure which can be virtually doubled when the large volunteer labour element is factored in. Ongoing public support is crucial so that future generations of steam enthusiasts and young engineers can be assured of experiencing the thrill of seeing a live steam locomotive at work.

For further information about the exciting 82045 project, contact the Trust at 'Highlea', 4 Southfield, Prestbury, Macclesfield, Cheshire SK10 4XF, or visit their informative website at www.82045.org.uk.

Chapter 10

BR STANDARD 'CLASS 2MT' 2-6-2T 'CLASS 2 TANK'

Newly introduced into traffic Darlington built BR Standard 2MT 2-6-2T No 84022 is pictured with a Rye to Ashford four coach local stopping train at Ham Street in March 1957. *D. C. Ovenden/Colour Rail*

BR Standard 2MT 2-6-2T No 84006 is pictured approaching Wellingborough station in 1960. Note the vacuum control equipment mounted on the side of the smokebox. *Rail Photoprints Collection*

It was logical that Ivatt's LMS 2-6-2T passenger tank locomotive (which was a tank version of the designer's Class 2 Mogul) should be adapted for inclusion in the BR Standard range. The 82000 series 2MT locomotives were in fact a tank version of the BR Standard 78000 series of tender engines.

Changes to the Ivatt design were minimal however the BR Standard features included boiler feed clack valves in the place of the LMS design top feed and the addition of external regulator rodding. The 2MT 2-6-2T boiler, which was designated as type BR8, was dimensionally the same as that of its LMS predecessor. Significantly the stated BR weight of both types was 63 tons 5 cwts, although in reality the Standard class 2 tanks were in fact slightly heavier at 66 tons 5 cwts.

The 1957 Darlington built batch was originally scheduled to be built at that works during 1953, but that order was changes was changed, mainly due to funding issues. The advancing proliferation of various types of railcars into service with British Railways effectively reduced the usefulness of the class; as a consequence further builds of the type were not contemplated.

In Traffic/Modifications

The class had wide route availability and proved to be easily serviced and able performers. The engines were at first fitted with vacuum control equipment in order to facilitate motor train (push pull) working which was later removed. In keeping with BR Standard constructional practice at that time the original dished ('I' section) coupling rods called for on the design specification were changed on later build engines to flat section (fish belly) coupling rods. The chosen livery was BR lined black although later in their working lives some of the class were repainted unlined black.

Disposal

All 35 locos were in traffic by the end of 1957 and the class remained intact until October 1963 when No 84012 was withdrawn after only 10 years and 1 month in traffic. The total in traffic was reduced to 20 engines by the end of 1964 and all the remaining members of the class were withdrawn before the end of 1965. None of the class survived into preservation however a 'new build' representative of the type was under construction in 2012.

BR Standard 'Class 2MT' 2-6-2T 'Class 2 Tank' class facts

2-6-2T BR Standard 'Class 2 Tank' - 30 locomotives built

Introduced: 1953-1957

Designer: Riddles. Parent office for design Derby

Company: British Railways

Weight: 63 ton 5 cwt

Tender Coal Capacity: 3 ton

Water Capacity: 1350 gallons

Driving Wheel: 5 foot diameter

Boiler Pressure: 200 psi superheated

Cylinders: 16½ inch diameter x 24 inch stroke

Tractive Effort: 18515lbf

Valve Gear: Walschaert piston valves

Ivatt's LMS 2-6-2T passenger tank locomotive (which was a tank version of the designer's Class 2 Mogul) was adapted for inclusion in the BR Standard range becoming the BR Standard 2MT 2-6-2T class in the 84000 number series. The obvious difference seen in these two images is the replacement of the LMS boiler

BR Standard 2MT 2-6-2T No 84026 is pictured whilst shunting vans at Stockport station in 1965. *Mike Stokes*

LMS Ivatt 2MT 2-6-2T No 41249 is pictured on shed at Willesden (1A) in 1959. *Mike Stokes*

top feed with a clack valve arrangement. Note also the fall plate ahead of the cylinders, the BR standard chimney and the modified cab at gutter level on the BR design. The Ivatt design had a metal ladder on the rear of the coal tender which on the BR designed loco was replaced by a series of well positioned grab rails.

BR standard 2MT No 84014 was pictured at Stockport Edgeley (9B) in the company of sister loco No 84026 in December 1964. *Mike Stokes Collection*

Standard Class 2 2-6-2T build details

Loco numbers	Build location	Year
84000–84019	Crewe	1953
84020–84029*	Darlington	1957

*Locomotive No 84029 was the last of 2,269 steam loco to be built at Darlington Works.

Original locomotive regional allocations

London Midland Region

84000–84019

Southern Region

84020–84029

BR Standard 2MT 2-6-2T No 84026 is pictured at Ore with a service ex Margate in May 1958. *L. Rowe/Colour Rail*

With the chimney covered to protect the smoke box from the elements, BR Standard 2MT 2-6-2T No 84005 is pictured in gently falling snow at Kentish Town depot (14B) in January 1963. *Rail Photoprints Collection*

BR Standard 2MT 2-6-2T No 84006 is pictured at Higham Ferrers station in May 1959. *K.C.H. Fairey/Colour Rail*

BR Standard 2MT 2-6-2T No 84001 is pictured in a filthy exterior condition outside the 1957 built running shed at Llandudno Junction (6G) in May 1963.

BR Standard 2MT 2-6-0 No 84030 – New Build Locomotive

Almost on the 45th anniversary of the last BR Class 2 tank locomotive being cut for scrap a proposed reincarnation of the type received a real boost at the Bluebell Railway's locomotive works when the completed frames for 'new build' engine No 84030 were officially unveiled.

The rescued hulk of BR Standard 2MT 2-6-0 tender engine No 78059 has become the donor loco for the planned new build. That loco, which was left decaying at Woodham Brothers Barry scrapyard for some time was minus a tender. At the Bluebell that loco is no longer referred to as No 78059 but as its new form No 84030, in 2012 no completion date was set for the project but importantly the eagerly anticipated transformation was underway.

The frames for the new build '2MT' 2-6-2T No 84030 stand inside Sheffield Park Works (Bluebell Railway) in January 2012. This view looking from the bunker end clearly shows the new extension and rear buffer beam fitted in order to turn the former tender engine into a tank locomotive. *Ian Wright*

The team are creating a new example of a class that worked on the London Midland and Southern Regions of British Railways, and which would otherwise not exist. This type of tank engine with coal capacity of 3 tons and a 1350 gallon water tanks will prove to be extremely useful to preserved railways in the future. In BR usage the class were extremely effective and were described by steam engineers of that time as being efficient and reliable machines.

Visit http://www.bluebellrailway.co.uk/bluebell/locos/84030.html for news of the project or contact tony@tonyrail.fsnet.co.uk.

Donor engine No 78059 as it was on arrival at Sheffield Park (Bluebell Railway) just after the engine's arrival from Barry on 23rd May 1983. *84030 Group*

Chapter 11

BR STANDARD 'CLASS 9F' 2-10-0

BR Standard 9F 2-10-0 No 92049 (a Crewe built engine which entered service in March 1955) is pictured outside Chester, just over 10 years later whilst heading a train for Shotton along the North Wales Coast route in September 1965. *Keith Langston*

The Mighty 9F's

By far most powerful, and many would argue the most successful BR Standard type was the 'Class 9F' 2-10-0, Brighton designed freight locomotives. Engine number 92220 holds the distinction of being the last steam locomotive built by British Railways, painted in lined green livery and given a GWR style copper topped chimney it was rolled out of Swindon Works in March 1960, and to mark that poignant occasion the loco was named 'EVENING STAR'

In the immediate post WWII period the ex 'WD Austerities' and Stanier 8F locomotives had helped to fulfil BR's need for powerful freight locomotives, but there was a perceived need to replace/augment the ageing members of those types with a powerful BR Standard design. The original BR Standard thinking behind the design requirements for a heavy freight locomotive was an engine in the 2-8-2 Mikado style with a probable power rating of 8F. If built that class of engines would have had a boiler, cylinders and other details in common with the BR Standard Britannia class 4-6-2 Pacific types.

BR Standard 9F locomotives were regularly diagrammed to work oil tank trains out of Stanlow Refinery (via the Helsby to Mouldsworth branch line in order to join the Cheshire Lines) An unidentified member of the class was pictured heading north through Delamere Forest in 1966. *Keith Langston*

No doubt the Mikado concept would have delivered a very useful mixed traffic engine, which with driving wheels of 5 foot 3 inch diameter would also have been capable of a good turns of speed when required. However Riddles and his team, whilst appraising what they saw as the networks likely heavy freight locomotive requirements for the future, settled on a 2-10-0 design with only 5 foot diameter driving wheels. Plain bearings were used on all engine wheels however the various types of tenders were fitted with roller bearing axleboxes.

The boiler design selected for the BR Standard 2-10-0 engines was not a copy of any other Standard class and was designated as type BR9. The 9F boiler was pitched high enough to allow the grate to adequately clear the rear coupled wheels (whilst remaining within the constraints of the L2 loading gauge requirement). The grate itself was flat over the rear half and then sloped towards the front. A design of non 'BR Standard' type regulator, which operated by way of a sliding grid throttle in the steam dome, was specified and it was activated by exterior rodding.

In Traffic

The locomotives were designed to haul the heaviest of freight trains at reasonably high speeds. In British Railways service they also worked passenger trains at speeds reported to be between 80 and 90mph, an incredible achievement for a small

BR Standard 9F 2-10-0 No 92244, a Cardiff Canton (88A) allocated loco at that time is pictured at Oxford depot (81F). This magnificent double chimney loco entered service in October 1958 and being withdrawn in December 1965 was only in BR service for 7 years and 3 months. *David Anderson*

diameter driving wheel 2-10-0 design. Locomotive of the class regularly worked fast passenger trains over the difficult Somerset & Dorset line in the final years before its closure.

This impressive class had only a short service life, but long enough to prove their worth. The original design 9F 2-10-0s were powerful, reliable and popular with the engine crews. The 21ft 8in wheelbase had to be capable of following tight curves and, to achieve this, the team designed the centre pair of driving wheels without flanges, whilst at the same time and in order to widen route availability kept the axle loading to only 15 tons 10cwt.

Real pulling power was the main asset of the Standard Class 9s. With great success they worked heavy, mineral, coal and general freight trains. The Tyne Dock-Consett workings were perhaps the hardest regular tasks ever undertaken by the class, and those iron ore trains could weigh up to 787 tons each. In addition they had to be hauled up gradients as steep as 1 in 35, a task that proved well within the capability of 9Fs when working in pairs. Nine of the original build Standard 9F 2-10-0s survived into preservation.

Loco No 92022 and other Franco – Crosti engines are seen under construction at Crewe Works during an open day event in March 1955. *Rail Photoprints Collection*

Disposal

By the end of 1954 there were 32 of the class in service but all 251 were not in service together until the March 1960. The numbers in traffic stayed that way until the first 6 engines of the class were withdrawn in May 1964; they were Nos 92034, 92169/70/71 and 92175/76. By the end of 1966 there were 125 of the class still in traffic however that number reduced to only 16 engines by the end of 1967. The last BR Standard 9F locomotives to be withdrawn were Nos 92077, 92160 and 92167 in July 1968.

The Franco – Crosti experiment

In 1955 the design team experimented with the Franco - Crosti boiler system, to hopefully save on coal and also make lower-quality coal usable, with the benefit of hindsight and collated performance data it was later judged that the experiment was a failure. The Crosti twin boiler locomotives had smaller fireboxes married to conventional tapered boilers 'on' the frames, which were located above smaller diameter pre-heat boilers located between the frames. Each boiler had a separate smoke box door. Draughting and exhaust systems were altered accordingly. The twin boiler system was developed in the 1930s by engineers Attilio Franco and Dr Piero Crosti who were at that time working for Italian State Railways (Ferrovie dello Stato-FS).

Basically the Franco – Crosti system uses the heat remaining in the locomotives exhaust gases to preheat the main boilers water supply. The heat exchanger arrangement, which is in effect a secondary boiler designed to raise the temperature of the feed water, but not to produce steam. Therefore the energy in the exhaust gases is put to good use as the preheated water is then fed, at full boiler pressure, into the conventional boiler.

A Crosti engines conventional chimney is only used during the lighting up process, with exhaust firebox gasses exiting the chimney in the normal manner. Once the boiler starts to produce steam the normal chimney is closed and the hot gasses are diverted through the feed water heater and leave the engine via a long slim multiple blast pipe located on the side of the boiler.

After loco No 92019 was completed in October 1954 production at Crewe was halted for a short while whilst the necessary engineering alterations were made by the BR Standard design team. The first BR built Franco – Crosti locos, No 92020 - 92023 entered revenue earning service in March 1955 being initially allocated to Wellingborough (15A). Over the following 4 months of that year the remaining Crewe built Crosti locos No 92024 – 92029 were also allocated to that depot.

The anticipated fuel savings and increases in performance levels were well below acceptable levels. Additionally the locomotives suffered from corrosion problems in the tube water heaters, chimney and final smokebox. Consequently in 1958 the 9F Franco – Crosti venture was abandoned by BR. The 10 twin boilered engines were at first laid up but over the following couple of years were

Franco – Crosti Standard 9F locomotive No 92028 is pictured near to Chester in 1958. The locomotives conventional chimney is only used during the lighting up procedure. The multi blast pipe exhaust is located beneath the odd looking smoke deflector on the side of the loco. Note the two smokebox doors and also the grab handle close to the chimney to facilitate closure etc. *Keith Langston Collection*

converted back to conventional operation (the pre-heat boiler was left in situ but sealed off).

These engines retained their Crosti look through out their working lives and consequently they were not fitted with smoke deflectors. The full working order weight of the reconfigured engines was recorded at 83.6 tons, slightly lighter than the normal BR Standard 9Fs. After being converted back to single boiler operation the engines were then considered capable of delivering performances akin to locomotive of an 8F power rating.

Other Modifications

Unlike some other BR Standard types the 2-10-0 locomotives were fitted with flat (fish bellied) coupling rods from the start. After the first 16 locomotives had entered traffic it was found necessary to modify the regulator sliding grid throttle arrangement as it was found to be less that satisfactory. The throttles proved hard to close and as a consequence caused excessive slipping at slow speeds when hauling heavy loads.

Franco – Crosti Standard 9F locomotive No 92020 (the first of the kind in service) is pictured at Wellingborough (15A) in 1955. *K.C.H. Fairey/Colour Rail*

Two ashpan doors were later fitted in order to facilitate ash raking they were located at the front and back of the firebox, above the rear coupled wheels. Some of the class were either built, or re-built with double chimneys and those engines were Nos 92000/1, No 92003, 92006, Nos 92165–92167, 92178 and Nos 92183–92249.

Ten of the class were fitted with pairs of Westinghouse air pumps to facilitate working hopper doors on mineral trains (specifically iron ore trains in the North East of England) those locomotives were No's 92060–92066 and No's 92097–92099. The pumps were located midway along the running plate. The air pump fitted locos were all initially allocated to Tyne Dock depot (then 54B).

Loco No 92250 was fitted with a Giesl oblong shaped ejector in the place of a normal chimney. This specific type of blast pipe was intended to reduce coal consumption. Under test conditions the Giesl system results were described as disappointing, to that end no other members of the class were similarly converted however No 92250 ran with the system for all of its working life.

Crewe 1958 built engines Nos 92165 to 92167 were experimentally fitted with mechanical stokers, initially those engines were allocated to Saltley depot (21A).

The last BR Standard 9F 2-10-0 to remain at Barry was No 92245 which was pictured there in 2008. *Keith Langston*

BR Standard 9F 2-10-0 No 92133 on shed at Heaton Mersey in 1966 (then 9F). Note the open ashpan doors. *Keith Langston Collection*

The aim was to increase the firing rate well beyond that of a single fireman, and in doing so raise the rate of evaporation to a level high enough to enable the engines to work fully fitted freight trains at faster speeds, with loads of 50 or more 16 ton capacity wagons. The chosen piece of equipment was of American Berkley design which to work properly required a supply of specially crushed coal. In traffic the experiment did not constantly achieve a desired level of improvement and the mechanical stokers were removed in 1962.

Interestingly one of those engines survived (in hand fired form) as the last Standard 9F in British Railways service, No 92167 was not withdrawn until July 1968. And therein hangs a tale. The loco carried out its last duties as a makeshift 2-8-2 having had the rear set of coupling rods removed. Effectively that was perhaps the nearest the standard design team ever got to fulfilling the Mikado proposal!

Various types of tenders were used (refer to separate table) and the choice of type married to a particular engine was mainly dependent upon the locos regional allocation.

All five 6 wheel tender variations were of a later BR pattern which incorporated fall plates to suit the loco cab design and were intended to reduce draughts. All the tenders were fitted with roller bearing axleboxes.

Franco – Crosti Standard 9F locomotive No 92022 after being converted back to single boiler configuration is seen at Stockport Edgeley Junction in July 1967 with a long train of fitted tanks. Note that the secondary boiler door has been sealed of and a fabricated step fitted onto the buffer beam. *Keith Langston*

BR Standard 'Class 9F' 2-10-0 'Class 9F' class facts

2-10-0 BR Standard 'Class 9F' - 251 locomotives built

Introduced: 1954–1960

Designer: Riddles. Parent office for design Brighton

Company: British Railways

Weight Loco: 86 ton 14 cwt Franco Crosti type 90 ton 4 cwt

Tender Coal Capacity: Refer to separate panel

Water Capacity: Refer to separate panel

Driving Wheel: 5 foot diameter

Boiler Pressure: 250 psi superheated

Cylinders: 20 inch diameter x 28 inch stroke

Tractive Effort: 39670lbf

Valve Gear: Walschaert piston valves

Tender types originally allocated to BR Standard 9F 2-10-0

Loco Numbers	Tender type	Coal Capacity	Water Capacity
92000–92009	BR1G	7 ton	5000 gallon
92010–92014	BR1F	7 ton	5625 gallon
92015–92019	BR1C	9 ton	4725 gallon
92020–92029	BR1B	7 ton	4725 gallon
92030–92044	BR1F	7 ton	5625 gallon
92045–92059	BR1C	9 ton	4725 gallon
92060–92066	BR1B	7 ton	4725 gallon
92067–92076	BR1F	7 ton	5625 gallon
92077–92086	BR1C	9 ton	4725 gallon
92087–92096	BR1F	7 ton	5625 gallon
92097–92099	BR1B	7 ton	4725 gallon
92100–92139	BR1C	9 ton	4725 gallon
92140–92149	BR1F	7 ton	5625 gallon
92150–92164	BR1C	9 ton	4725 gallon
92165–92167	BR1K	9 ton	4325 gallon
92168–92202	BR1F	7 ton	5625 gallon
92203–92250	BR1G	7 ton	5000 gallon

An interesting BR Standard front end comparison, to the left is preserved BR Standard Britannia No 70000 and to the right preserved BR 9F No 92203 BLACK PRINCE. *Keith Langston*

Standard Class 9F 2-10-0 build details

Loco Numbers	Build Location	Year
92000–92019	Crewe	1954
92020–92029*	Crewe	1955
92030–92086	Crewe	1954/56
92087–92096	Swindon	1956/57
92097–92177	Crewe	1956/58
92178–92220	Swindon	1959/60
92221–92250	Crewe	1958

*Built as Franco Crosti locomotives

Original locomotive regional allocations

Western Region

92000–92007, 92203–92250

London Midland Region

92008–92009, 92015–92029, 92045–92059, 92077–92086, 92100–92139, 92150–92167

Eastern Region

92010–92014, 92030–92044, 92067–92076, 92087–92096, 92140–92149, 92168–92202

North Eastern Region

92060–92066, 92097–92099

The BR 9F 2-10-0 wheel arrangement with flangeless centre driving wheel can be a appreciated in this image of preserved loco No 92203 BLACK PRINCE, which was taken at LNWR Heritage Ltd Crewe. *Keith Langston*

BR Standard 9F 2-10-0 No 92133 seen hard a work with a southbound fitted freight at Moore on the WCML in April 1967, another member of the class can be seen in the far distance with a northbound train of oil tanks. *Keith Langston*

BR Standard 9F 2-10-0 No 92112 is pictured passing through Delamere Forest with a train of oil tanks ex Stanlow Oil Refinery, in 1966. Note the DMU on the opposite track operating the Manchester–Chester Cheshire Lines service. *Keith Langston*

Franco – Crosti Standard 9F locomotive No 92026, after being converted back to single boiler configuration is pictured on passenger duty. The loco is seen hauling the afternoon running of the Chester–Crewe leg of the LCGB Severn & Dee Railtour, 26 February 1967. This loco was withdrawn in the November of that year. *Keith Langston*

BR Standard 9F 2-10-0 No 92203 is pictured at Foxhall Junction, Didcot (West Curve) with a Swindon–Birmingham express freight train in this 1961 image. *David Anderson*

BR Standard 9F 2-10-0 No 92017, a Newton Heath (26A) allocated locomotive is pictured passing through Manchester Victoria station with a special passenger working in 1958. *Mike Stokes Collection*

Franco–Crosti Standard 9F locomotive No 92020, after being converted back to single boiler configuration is pictured on shed at Warrington Dallam (8B) in July 1967, just 3 months before being withdrawn from service. *Keith Langston*

BR Standard 9F 2-10-0 No 92021, a re-converted ex Franco-Crosti loco. The 15A (Wellingborough) allocated loco is pictured on shed at Oxford (81F) in April 1962. *David Anderson*

BR Standard 9F 2-10-0 No 92109 pictured when in 'full cry' with a heavy freight train on the outskirts of Swinton in 1958. *Mike Stokes Collection*

Franco – Crosti Standard 9F locomotive No 92029 pictured outside the main shed building at Wellingborough (15A) in January 1957. *K.C.H. Fairey/Colour Rail*

BR Standard 9F 2-10-0 No 92138 is seen passing through Wellingborough station with a long mixed freight train. *K.C.H. Fairey/Colour Rail*

Franco–Crosti Standard 9F locomotive No 92027, after being converted back to single boiler configuration is pictured on shed at Heaton Mersey in 1960 (then 9F). Note that the BR Standard 9Fs had a 21ft 8in wheelbase but still need to be capable of following tight curves, to achieve this, the team designed the centre pair of driving wheels without flanges. *Mike Stokes Collection*

BR Standard 9F 2-10-0 No 92245 is seen at Foxhall Junction, Didcot whilst in charge of a Birmingham–Swindon freight working. *David Anderson*

Under construction preserved Crewe built BR Standard 9F is seen in the workshops of LNWR Heritage Ltd Crewe.
Keith Langston

Thunder in the forest! BR Standard 9F 2-10-0 No 92152 disturbs the peace and quiet of Delamere Forest on the former Cheshire Lines Conference (CLC) Chester-Manchester route, as the loco heads north in May 1957 with a train of oil tanks from Stanlow Refinery. The train had reached the CLC line via a now removed single line connection between Helsby (Chester – Warrington route) and Mouldsworth (north of Chester). *Keith Langston Collection*

Preserved BR Standard 2-10-0 9F locomotives

Number	In Traffic	Builder	Ex BR	Home Base
92134	May 1957	Crewe	December 1966	LNWR Crewe
92203	April 1959	Swindon	November 1967	Gloucestershire & Warwickshire Railway
92207	June 1959	Swindon	December 1964	Shillingstone Station
92212	September 1959	Swindon	January 1968	Mid Hants Railway
92214	October 1959	Swindon	August 1965	North Yorkshire Moors Railway
92219	January 1960	Swindon	August 1965	Midland Railway Centre
92220	March 1960	Swindon	March 1965	NRM York
92240	October 1958	Crewe	August 1965	Bluebell Railway
92245	November 1958	Brighton	December 1964	Barry Island Railway

BR 9F 2-10-0 preserved locomotives status in January 2012

92134 – Active restoration project, the loco was in a partially restored condition, but was minus a tender.

92203 – Named *BLACK PRINCE* in preservation, serviceable engine, has visited several heritage lines.

92207 – Active restoration www.shillingstone.addr.com/the_morning_star_story.htm

92212 – A serviceable engine, steams regularly.

92214 – Named *COCK OF THE NORTH* in preservation, a serviceable engine.

92219 – Scrap condition www.thorneywood.btinternet.co.uk/mlsteamloco/br9f.htm

92220 – Has steamed extensively, currently on static display.

92240 – Has steamed extensively, currently on static display.

92245 – Still in scrap condition.

May 1986 and preserved BR Standard 9F 2-10-0 No 92220 EVENING STAR is pictured on the outskirts of Chester, whilst on special charter train duty. As the last standard gauge steam locomotive built by British Railways No 92220 was immediately scheduled for preservation. The freight loco was painted in full BR 'Passenger Green' livery and a GWR style copper top adorned its double chimney. This loco was the shortest lived member of the class in BR service but after withdrawal was used extensively on railtour work. In January 2012 the National Collection loco was listed as 'out of service' but was on static display at the National Railway Museum. *Both images Keith Langston*

On a very damp 27 January 2002 preserved BR Standard 9F 2-10-0 No 92212 emits the kind of exhaust beloved by railway photographers as the loco works hard climbing up Burrs Incline on the East Lancashire Railway with a Heywood- Rawtenstall service. *Fred Kerr*

No 92212 is seen again, this time at the Great Central Railway whilst hauling an authentic rake of 'Windcutter' wagons. The colloquial name 'Windcutter' was used for unfitted freight trains which used to run from Annesley collection yard, which handled coal shipments from several Nottinghamshire collieries in BR days and was served by the ex Great Central Railway.(these mineral wagons were also referred to as 'Annesley Cutters'). *David Gibson*

BR Standard 9F 2-10-0 No 92220 is pictured on the Settle - Carlisle route whilst on Cumbrian Mountain Express duty in April 1984. *Fred Kerr*

Preserved BR Standard 9F 2-10-0 No 92203 is seen hard at work with a demonstration infrastructure train on the Gloucester & Warwickshire Railway during a 2008 Spring Gala event. *Pete Sherwood*

Preserved BR Standard 9F 2-10-0 No 92214 is pictured at the East Lancashire Railway. Above The loco is seen departing Bury Bolton Street station with a Heywood-Rawtenstall service. Below. The 9F is seen approaching Irwell Vale with a train for Rawtenstall. The smoke in the background is from BR Standard 4-6-2 No 71000 which was assisting at the rear. *Both images Fred Kerr*

Still in scrap condition as we entered 2012 the hulk of BR Standard 9F 2-10-0 No 92245 (one of the so called 'Barry 10') is pictured at Barry Island Railway. *Keith Langston*

Preserved BR Standard 9F 2-10-0 No 92207 (a medium term restoration project in 2012) is pictured prior to being rescued from Woodham Brothers scrap yard, Barry Glamorgan. *Keith Langston*

Preserved BR Standard 9F 2-10-0 No 92203 BLACK PRINCE makes a fine sight departing from Irwell Vale on the East Lancashire Railway with a Bury- Rawtenstall service in April 1993. *Keith Langston*

Preserved BR Standard 9F 2-10-0 No 92134 (a long term restoration project) is pictured during the 2005 Great Gathering Event back in Crewe Works where she was built in April 1957. *Keith Langston*

The sheer size of the BR Standard 9F 2-10-0 class can really be appreciated when studying this image taken of No 92203 masquerading as class mate No 92206 during a visit to Barrow Hill roundhouse railway centre in July 2001. *Fred Kerr*

Preserved BR Standard 9F 2-10-0 No 92203 2-10-0 BLACK PRINCE seen working hard at Deeside on the Llangollen Railway during a March 1998 visit. *Fred Kerr*

Preserved BR Standard 9F 2-10-0 BLACK PRINCE hard at work is a magnificent sight even in Lancashire drizzle, the loco is seen at Sommerseat on the East Lancashire Railway in Apri 1995. *Fred Kerr*

Voluminous display of smoke and steam as preserved BR Standard 9F 2-10-0 No 92212 roars up Burrs Incline on the East Lancashire Railway, early on a misty morning in September 2001. *Fred Kerr*

Preserved BR Standard 9F 2-10-0 No 92212 has visited several preserved railways but is pictured on home territory at Aleresford, Mid-Hants Railway. *Fred Kerr*

Preserved BR Standard 9F 2-10-0 No 92220 EVENING STAR is pictured with a summer 1985 White Rose working passing Delamere Station en route to Chester (Ex York) on the former CLC. *Keith Langston*

Chapter 12

R A RIDDLES – WAR DEPARTMENT (WD) AUSTERITY LOCOMOTIVES

Engines for wartime

In September 1939 R.A. Riddles was appointed to the newly created position of Director of Transportation Equipment for the Ministry of Supply, on the very day that war broke out between Britain and Germany. He was given a comprehensive role which included overseeing the manufacture of diverse items of equipment all seen as essential to the war effort, the list included 'Bailey Bridges', cranes, Mulberry harbours and even Jerricans! As far as the railways were concerned his brief was clear, large numbers of locomotives were needed to help the war effort he had to select or create the type(s) and whilst being mindful of the impending scarcity of raw material and resources get them built quickly.

His first thought was to repeat the emergency actions taken during WW1 and make available quantities of Robinson GCR designed 2-8-0s to the military. Amongst his reasons for discounting that possibility was their excessive width (over the outside cylinders) which restricted route availability. The War Department had already placed an order for 240 Stanier designed 8F 2-8-0 engines which should have been shipped to France; however the famous retreat from Dunkirk necessitated the cancellation of that plan. Later the Stanier 8Fs were re-directed to other theatres of war where they performed with distinction.

WD 2-8-0 8F No 90733 is seen under test at LNWR Heritage Ltd, Crewe after a 2007 restoration to working condition. This loco was WD 79257, it worked in Holland as number 4464 and then in Sweden as number 1931. The BR number it carries in restoration is a fictitious one as the BR number series ended at 90732. *Keith Langston*

The sheer size of the Hunslet WD 'Austerity' 0-6-0ST type can be gauged in this picture of the beautifully restored example No 68030 when seen coupled to Ex GWR 2-8-0T 5224, at the Churnet Valley Railway. The number given to the 0-6-0ST is simply representative of the engine it portrays as the Hunslet Engine Co Ltd built loco which carried that BR number was scrapped in October 1962. *Keith Langston*

Shunting engines

The Ministry of Supply had already selected a shunting locomotive design to compliment the fleet of Wartime General Duties Locomotives which Riddles was asked to create, that loco was a powerful 'Austerity' 0-6-0ST originated by the Hunslet Engine Company, which Riddles design team modified to suit WD requirements. The Saddle tank had the look of a traditional industrial locomotive but was in all respects a 'big' little engine. With a power rating of 4F the Austerity tank, which had 4 foot 3 inch diameter driving wheels, justified the criteria of having almost universal route availability.

Hunslet/Riddles 0-6-0ST J94 class facts

0-6-0 ST MOS (War Department) 'Class 4F' - 75 locomotives purchased 1946

Introduced: 1943–1946

Designer: Riddles and Hunslet Engine Company

Company: Ministry of Supply/LNER

Weight: 48 ton 5 cwt

Wheels: 4 foot 3 inches diameter

Boiler Pressure: 170 psi superheated

Cylinders: 18 inch diameter x 26 inch stroke

Tractive Effort: 23870lbf

Valve Gear: Stephenson slide valves

The Hunslet/Riddles 0-6-0ST was built in great numbers between 1943 and 1946. Not only the Hunslet Engine Co Ltd but also by Andrew Barclay Sons & Co Ltd, W G Bagnall Ltd, Hudswell Clarke & Co Ltd, Robert Stephenson & Hawthorns Ltd and Vulcan Foundry Ltd. From the several hundred built many were sold at the end of the war to industrial concerns, docks, mines, steel works etc in addition the LNER bought 75 of the engines (numbered them as 8006-8080) with the class

WG Bagnall Ltd built ex WD 0-6-0ST shunting loco seen as BR 68057 at West Hartlepool (51C) in 1960. *Keith Langston*

identity 'J94'. In 1948 they became British Railways stock with the number series 68006- 68080. As steam on BR was discontinued and preserved railways were created the Austerity 0-6-0ST design proved ideal for their purpose and approximately 50 examples survived to work again, that number includes two of the LNER batch, numbers 68077 and 68078.

WD 2-8-0 freight locomotives

The accuracy of the word 'Austerity' as applied to the WD engines is easily explained by the examination of a few facts. The Stanier 2-8-0 8F's used approximately 22 tons of steel castings per engine whilst the WD 2-8-0 8F's were constructed using only 2 ½ tons of steel castings. For example cast iron was used for the cylinders, blast pipe, smoke box saddle, chimney and front end cylinder covers. Parallel boilers and round topped fireboxes were a far cheaper option than the Stanier tapered boiler and Belpaire firebox design. North British Locomotive Ltd assembled the first WD 2-8-0 in only 10 working days, thus creating a record for the firm when the first WD 8F was out-shopped on January 16th 1943. Records show that the 'Austerities' were built at almost twice the rate at which it had been possible to build the Stanier 8F 2-8-0 locomotives.

Between 1943 and 1946 a total of 934 WD 2-8-0 MOD (WD) 'Austerity' locomotives were built by North British Locomotive Co Ltd and Vulcan Foundry Ltd. Many saw service in France, Belgium and Holland during WWII.

From delivery of the first loco until October 1944 all the 2-8-0's in service were initially 'loaned' by the War Department to the UK various railway companies.

WD Class 8F 2-8-0 build details

WD numbers	Build location	Year
7000–7049	North British	1943
7050–7059	Vulcan Foundry	1943
7060–7109	Vulcan Foundry	1943
7110–7149	Vulcan Foundry	1943
7450–7479	Vulcan Foundry	1943
7150–7449	North British	1943/44
7460–7509	Vulcan Foundry	1943/44
800–879	North British	1944
8510–8624	North British	1944/45
8625–8671	Vulcan Foundry	1944
8672–8718	Vulcan Foundry	1944
9177–9219	Vulcan Foundry	1944
9220–9262	Vulcan Foundry	1944/45
9263–9313	Vulcan Foundry	1945

Banbury (84C) allocated WD 2-8-0 8F No 90315 on shed at Oxford (81F) in May 1961. *David Anderson*

However starting in November 1944, and after the Western Allies invaded France, WD 8F locomotives were gradually shipped to mainland Europe.

Ministry of Supply War Department (MoS WD) loco No 7337 was severely damaged at Soham in Cambridgeshire on 1 June 1944 when an ammunition wagon exploded. The quick and heroic action of the engine crew almost certainly saved the village. Loco Driver Gimbert noticed the first wagon of his ammunition train was on fire, and he promptly stopped the train. The locomotive crew disconnected the wagon from the rest of the train and thereafter started to draw the burning vehicle forward and importantly away from the village.

Tragically as his locomotive passed the signal box the burning wagon exploded, creating a 66 foot diameter crater. The huge detonation of ammunition destroyed both the station and stationmaster's house. Fireman Nightall and Signalman Bridgers both suffered fatal injuries, driver Gimbert survived but was seriously injured. Nightall and Gimbert were both awarded the LNER Medal and the George Cross in recognition of their selfless for their actions. The locomotive was later fitted with a new boiler, generally repaired and returned to service.

A permanent memorial was unveiled on Saturday 2 June 2007 by HRH Prince Richard, Duke of Gloucester followed by a service in St. Andrew's Church, Soham. The memorial is constructed of Portland Stone with a bronze inlay depicting interpretive artwork of the damaged train as well as text detailing the incident.

Built by Vulcan Foundry Ltd in 1944 WD 8F 2-8-0 No 90624 is pictured in charge of an Up Motherwell - Carlisle freight on 18 April 1959. *David Anderson*

Final Disposition of the class after conclusion of war time duties

LNER*	200 locos
BR	533 locos
Holland**	184
Kowloon-Canton Rly	12 locos
WD retained	2
Collision damaged	3
Missing***	1
Total	935 locos

*The LNER purchased 200 engines in 1946 (became Class 07) later taken into BR stock.

**Excludes 53 transferred away in June 1946 in exchange for 53 8F 2-10-0 class engines. Thereafter 52 eventually transferred to BR.

*** Loco WD No 79189 cannot be accounted for after leaving Nederlandse Spoorwegen (NR)

MOD (War Department) 2-8-0 'Class 8F' class facts

2-8-0 Ministry of Supply WD 'Class 8F' – 934 locomotives built

Introduced: 1943–1946

Designer: Riddles

Company: Ministry of Supply

Weight: 70 ton 5 cwt

Tender: 55 ton 10 cwt. Coal

Capacity: 9 tons, water capacity 5000 gallons

Driving Wheel: 4 foot 8 ½ inches diameter

Boiler Pressure: 225 psi superheated

Cylinders: 19 inch diameter x 28 inch stroke

Tractive Effort: 34215lbf

Valve Gear: Walschaert piston valves

Additionally in 1946/47 twelve of the class were shipped 'out east' to work on the Kowloon-Canton Railway, that being possible after the British had regained control of Hong Kong in 1945, which followed the defeat of Japan. Restoring the badly damaged railway to working order was at first placed in the hands of the military but was transferred back to civilian control in 1946.

Loco No 90763 WD Austerity 2-10-0 type built by the North British Locomotive Company pictured on shed at Carlisle Kingmoor (12A). *Keith Langston Collection*

In 1947 the LNER purchased 200 of the type which they re-listed as their class '07'. British Railways had 533 of the type on loan from the WD at the time of nationalisation which they then purchased outright before the end of 1948. The newly acquired locomotives were renumbered in 1949 in the BR number series 90000–90421 (Ex North British Locomotive Co Ltd - NBL engines) and 90422–90732 (Ex Vulcan Foundry Ltd – VF engines). Locomotive number 90732 (WD number 79312) carried the name VULCAN. None of the UK based WD 8F's survived all being scrapped before 1967; however a loco of the type repatriated from Europe (WD number 79257) is preserved in the UK as a working locomotive.

WD 2-10-0 freight locomotives

In 1943 a batch of 150 engines which were bigger version of the WD Austerity type and all were built by the North British Locomotive Company, that class had a 2-10-0 wheel arrangement. The locomotives extra set of wheels reduce their axle loading to 13 ½ tons (2-8-0 15¾ tons), thus allowing them to work over lighter laid track. One of the MOD WD 'Austerity' 2-10-0's (WD number 73755) had the distinction of being the 1000th WD loco built in the UK and shipped to Europe since D-Day, accordingly it was named LONGMOOR by the military.

In 1944 a batch of 20 of the 2-10-0s were shipped to the Middle East, a complement of 43 were sent to Belgium and 60 engines to Holland, by June of 1946 those 103 locos were all to be found working in the Netherlands. That left 20 in the Middle East plus 7 examples in military use and 20 on the LNER pre BR stock list. British Railways purchased the 25 UK based WD 8F 2-10-0 engines in 1948,

00 Gauge model of NS liveried loco No NS 4479, note Dutch style stove pipe chimney. *Keith Langston*

re-numbering them 90750–90774. Numbers 90773 and 90774 both carried the name, NORTH BRITISH; the names were removed by BR circa 1952.

On entering service on the BR network the WD 2-10-0 engines generated a great deal of interest amongst the railway fraternity. Running mainly in the BR Scottish Region the class were very successful in service and it is apparent that Riddles took his original inspiration for the BR Standard 9F 2-10-0 class from the Ministry of Supply 'Austerities.' All of the class were withdrawn before the end of 1962.

No Ex BR examples were preserved, but loco number 600 GORDON from the Longmoor Military Railway was saved and is loaned by the military to the Severn Valley Railway. In addition to the name plate No 600 also proudly carries the coat of arms of the Royal Engineers.

Two more WD 2-10-0 engines have been repatriated from Greece. One has been numbered 90775 (one higher than the last BR engine) and has occasionally carried the name STURDEE (as did No 601 before being numbered 90775) and that loco's home base is the North Norfolk Railway NNR).

The other is WD 2-10-0 is No 3672 which has been named DAME VERA LYNN. The loco's home base is at Grosmont on the North Yorkshire Moors Railway (NYMR). Loco WD No 73755 (NS 5085) survives in the Dutch Railway Museum (Nederlands Spoorwegmuseum) in Utrecht. It carried the nameplate LONGMOOR, after the Royal Engineer's base of that name, also the coat of arms of the Royal Engineers is displayed above the name. Three more examples of the class were in 2011 still listed as being in Greece, with 2 of those locos classified as operational.

MOD (War Department) 2-10-0 'Class 8F' class facts

2-10-0 Ministry of Supply WD 'Class 8F' - 150 locomotives built

Introduced: 1943

Designer: Riddles

Company: Ministry of Supply

Weight: 78 ton 6 cwt

Tender: 55 ton 10 cwt. Coal capacity 9 tons, water capacity 5000 gallons

Driving Wheel: 4 foot 8 ½ inches diameter

Boiler Pressure: 225 psi superheated

Cylinders: 19 inch diameter x 28 inch stroke

Tractive Effort: 34215lbf

Valve Gear: Walschaert piston valves

Disposal

Following the end of World War II and the formation of British Railways in 1948 a total of 733 WD 8F 2-8-0 locomotives were listed as BR stock. Although initially thought to have only a limited service life span these remarkable engines lasted well into the BR steam era, and were to be seen at work on all regions of the network. Scrapping started in 1958 with No 90083 being the first engine to be retired.

The first big cull was in 1962 with only 650 of the class still listed 'in service', at the end of that year. By the end of 1964 428 locos were still allocated to BR depots and that number was reduced to 227 by the end of 1965. The last year of operation for the BR 'Austerity' 8F 2-8-0s was 1967 when 123 remained in service, but none made it beyond the end of that year. Vulcan Foundry 1944 built loco No 90682 was the last member of the class to be withdrawn in September 1967.

Of the 150 WD 2-10-0 locomotives built 25 were listed as BR stock at the end of 1948. Those engines also had long service lives with the first 2 Nos 90753 and 90754 being withdrawn in July 1961. All the remaining members of the class were withdrawn before the end of 1962.

WD Austerity 2-8-0 No 90137 passes West Ruislip with a Neasden–Woodford Halse freight in September 1956. *C. R. L. Coles/Rail Photoprints Collection*

Preserved WD 2-8-0 loco No 600 GORDON, (ex WD 73651) seen hard a work with a demonstration freight train was based at the former operational Longmoor Military Railway and is now loaned by the military authorities to the Severn Valley Railway. *Keith Langston*

WD 8F 2-10-0 number 90762 is seen hard at work on Beattock Bank. Loco 90762 was built by NBL in July 1945 and withdrawn by BR in December 1962. *David Anderson*

WD 8F 2-8-0 No 90513 is pictured in the 1960s whilst working a very heavy freight train over the Blackford Hill section of the Edinburgh Suburban Line. *David Anderson*

WD 2-8-0 No 90682, a Normanton (55E) allocated loco is seen leaving Derby with a northbound freight in April 1963. *Rail Photoprints Collection*

Springs Branch Wigan (8F) allocated WD 2-8-0 No 90157 is seen approaching Wigan North Western station on the WCML with a northbound coal train in September 1963. *Jim Carter/Rail Photoprints Collection*

Note the large smokebox number on this WD 2-8-0 pictured in the winter snow at an unknown LNER location in 1947, prior to being renumbered. *Rail Photoprints Collection*

WD 2-8-0 No 90506 is seen in remarkable clean exterior condition for the period. Note the absence of a smokebox shedplate, the location is Gorton (9G) and the date was March 1963. *Rail Photoprints Collection*

WD 2-8-0 No 90721 is seen under the impressive coaling plant at Normanton (55E) in March 1967. Note the narrow gauge line and tipping ash disposal trucks. *Rail Photoprints Collection*

WD 2-8-0 No 90678 is seen minus a tender at Crewe Works in 1965. *Brian Robbins/Rail Photoprints Collection*

WD 2-8-0 No 90683 seen in ex works condition and minus a smokebox shed code plate at Doncaster shed (36A) in 1958. *Rail Photoprints Collection*

Circa 1960 and WD 2-8-0 No 90715 noses out of the main shed building at Newton Heath depot (then 26A) at this time the loco is minus a smokebox shed code plate. *Rail Photoprints Collection*

WD 2-10-0 No 90755 is pictured at Grangemouth depot (65F) on 1 March 1959. *David Anderson*

WD 2-10-0 No 90765 is seen in the company of an unidentified ex Caledonian Railway 0-6-0T at Grangemouth depot (65F) in May 1958. Note that the name Grangemouth is stencilled on the buffer beam. *David Anderson*

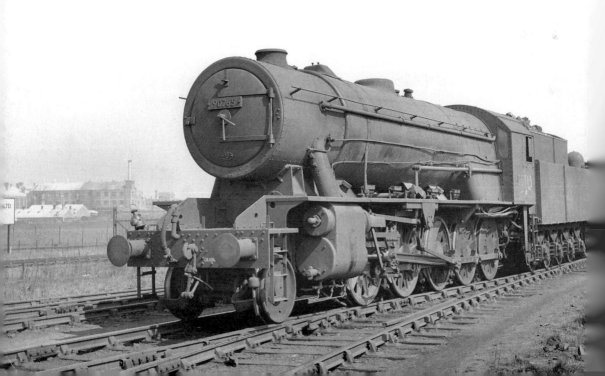

Preserved WD loco No 90733 is pictured at Townsend Fold on the East Lancashire Railway (ELR) in January 2010. *Fred Kerr*

Preserved WD loco No 90733 is pictured at Oakworth on the Keighley & Worth Valley Railway (KWVR) with a Keighley – Oxenhope demonstration freight train working in October 2007. *Fred Kerr*